DRAMATIC ENCOUNTERS

WILLIE L. GREEN

Order this book online at www.trafford.com
or email orders@trafford.com

Most Trafford titles are also available at major online book retailers.

Printed in the United States of America.

ISBN: 978-1-4907-4168-0 (sc)
ISBN: 978-1-4907-4170-3 (hc)
ISBN: 978-1-4907-4169-7 (e)

Library of Congress Control Number: 2014912285

Trafford rev. 07/23/2014

 www.trafford.com

North America & international
toll-free: 1 888 232 4444 (USA & Canada)
fax: 812 355 4082

CONTENTS

FOREWORD

This is not your basic water to wine book, but it covers a multitude of experiences in the life of the Author. We can sense the depth of his feelings in every word. His love of Christ explodes from the pages of this book. His premise, when you meet Jesus, your life will never be the same, your change will happen then and there. As we can see what happened to the Author when Jesus came into his life, he was never the same. Positive situations will begin to happen to you in your life, it's as if the light of day turns on and you begin to understand your call in life. When the Author's son encouraged him to incorporate his own life experiences into this book the tenor changed from a theological commentary to a personal testimony. The allusion to the painting of his Aunt's house and how everyone pitched in to help was inspiring. When you have Jesus in your life you become very driven. We live in a beautiful world, yet to survive we must know our real enemies. Our strong enemies are not people but invisible forces of darkness. Those forces formerly Allies who turned against our Lord. We know how the Devil took Jesus up to the top of the mountain and showed him the kingdoms of this world and offered it to Jesus if he would bow down to him. But Jesus used the word of God to overcome Satan. We can also overcome him with the power of the word of God. This powerful book illustrates all that we need, is to see Jesus as He truly is.

We know that salvation is from God through Jesus. Salvation was the plan of God since the great fall in the garden. Jesus became the very root of the plan when God decided to send his son to die for mankind on the cross and cleanse man with his blood. The word says we been bought with a price, and don't belong to ourselves. For we know the travails of Jesus, His desire is to be in our hearts. The word of God says that Jesus went about preaching the gospel and giving gifts to men, His greatest gift being Himself. The Author contends in this book , that worship is not about a place, but a person and the personal knowledge of God. We experience Him in the Holy Spirit that dwells in the hearts of men. Serving Him is like making an investment in a house or mortgage, the more time we put in, the value grows. This book really opened my eyes to the trials we have to face day to day, which pales when compared to the trials of Jesus. It is a very interesting and inspiring read; I hope you will enjoy this very well written book as much as I have. And glory to our Lord and Savior Jesus Christ. Amen

DENNIS MAXWELL

Rev. Dennis Maxwell is the Senior Pastor of Greater Works Ministry Miracle Center, Fort Lauderdale Florida

ACKNOWLEDGEMENTS

First of all, I want to honor the memory of my departed mentors, the late Dr Samuel Gordon, Chancellor of United Bible College and Seminary that accepted me as a novice preacher, honed me into a vessel useful to the Master; The late Dr Fred L. Maxwell, Pastor of St. John Missionary Baptist Church who licensed and ordained me and trusted his pulpit to me as I grew as a minister of the gospel; The late Rev. B.J. Wilson, who opened his heart to me as well as his bible explaining the nuances of obscure passages of scripture, making the Word of God come alive to me; The late Rev. Vincent B. Holmes, whose early instruction catapulted me from the pew to the harvest; The late Deacon Andrew Wade, whose authenticity made the transformation into a man of God seem as natural as breathing; the late Deacon Joe Maxwell whose gave me the oral history of my family solidifying my entrance into the family business, which is the gospel ministry.

I also want to thank Rev. Dr. Richard Bishop, my pastor, whose support and friendship means more to me than words can convey; The Rev. Dr. Walter Monroe, my seminary professor whose lectures on textual criticisms haunt me until this day; The Rev. Alex Linzy, my cousin and my "Rock" who encouraged me every step of the way on my Christian journey; also Minister David Thornton, my son in the ministry. I also want to thank my former student Taqueria Jones, whose constant prodding would not allow this project to cease nor let me lay down my pen, but most importantly, I want to thank my wife of twenty four years, Daisy for sticking by me and not getting too frustrated when I worked until the wee hours of the morning. She kept a hedge of protection around me as this labor of love took shape and would not allow any distractions or interruptions as I worked. I could not have done this without you.

Rev. Dr. Willie L. Green Jr.

Rev. Dr. Willie L. Green was born in Ft. Sill Oklahoma as an Army Brat and grew up in Orlando Florida. He graduated from Maynard Evans High School in 1973 and later attended Valencia Community College where he earned his Associate of Arts degree. He earned his BSBA from University of Central Florida with a major in Accounting in 1983. While attending UCF, he was employed part-time at Churches Fried Chicken who immediately promoted him into their management program upon graduation. He went through the ranks from team member, to assistant manager, General Manager, Training Manager and Area Manager.

Dr. Green came to faith in Christ in 1984 and began his ministry career serving as a Deacon at St. John Missionary Baptist Church in Orlando. While serving in the Diaconate, He soon realized that God was preparing him for the pastoral ministry. Shortly after announcing his call to the gospel ministry, he became licensed under the late Rev. Dr. Fred L. Maxwell and ordained in 2000. Rev. Green enrolled in United Bible College and Theological Seminary, where he attended from 1996 to 1998, graduating with a Master of Theology degree. Dr. Green received some additional training at New Orleans Baptist Theological Seminary. He served as the President of the United Bible College National Alumni Association from 1999 to 2002 and College Treasurer and Board Member from 2000 to 2003. Rev. Green was conferred the degree of Honorary Doctor of Humane Letters from United Bible College of Lakeland in May of 2008. Dr. Green was a founding Board Member of Grand

Avenue Economic CDC in Orlando which converted two hotels into permanent housing for homeless individuals. He served as Treasurer from its inception in 1992 until 2000.

Dr. Green is the founding pastor of Eternal Life Christian Fellowship and currently serves on the ministry staff of Agape Assembly Baptist Church and as Director of Adult Education in the Agape Christian Academy High School. Dr. Green is the editor of the blog www.buildinggreatdads.com, whose mission is to empower men with the tools to become more effective fathers.

INTRODUCTION

On our life's journey, we meet a lot of people, most of whom have little bearing on the quality or direction of our lives. It is a fact that not every personal contact is significant. Like ships passing in the night, we approach individuals from different directions and head toward our destinations without giving them any regard. While many of life's encounters are just as the passing ships, there are some exceptions. Often times, we encounter people who make such an impact on our lives that we are forever changed by them. `

This book explores a series of **Dramatic Encounters,** from the Gospel of St. John where a variety of persons come into contact with the Lord Jesus, and these contacts have a profound impact on their lives. Webster defines drama as: A poem or composition representing a picture of human life, and accommodated to action. These human characters come from divers backgrounds, with a variety of issues and hang-ups, but one thing they all have in common, when they encounter the Savior, the status quo of their lives is severely interrupted. The hidden recesses of their hearts are exposed to the light of day and the power of His presence always produces a response. It is impossible to be in the presence of Christ without being affected by Him.

I chose to use John's gospel as a backdrop for this book, and like the Evangelist John, when he wrote of Jesus, I thought of writing it in the third person. The evangelist always, with one exception (the Book of Revelation) referred to himself that way, (eg., the other disciple or the disciple whom the Lord loved). Upon the advice of my youngest son Virgil, urging me to interject my own story within this story, I decided to change my approach and do just that. Virgil made such a strong case; I was compelled to do the revision. In his opinion, my own testimony belonged in this book. My argument was that this book was about those characters in the scripture that had dramatic encounters with Jesus that changed their lives and was not about me. Virgil countered, "Didn't you have a dramatic encounter with Him that changed your life?" "It would fit right in." "I know your story, and you could easily weave it into the tapestry of this book, because it belongs there," He said. Subsequently, I relented, therefore in many passages, whosoever became "me" and the author became "I".

When I reflect upon my own life, I have always been surprised the Lord would love me at all, which explains why my standard charge to every new convert has been to read one chapter a day of John's Gospel for twenty one days with the anticipation that doing so would be life altering. With all the mistakes I'd made, promises broken and pledges violated, I wondered aloud, "how could I experience the love of God?" Nevertheless, I do and want others to do the same. With the assurance that there is no condemnation of those who are His, I found it easy to take Jesus at his Word. As the reader accompanies me on my journey, I anticipate that the reader would be as profoundly impacted as I've been. In addition to featured biblical texts in boxes, I interjected the biblical narratives directly into the text with the use of bold lettering to allow the reader to easily follow this book with an open bible.

With each introduction, with every encounter, these characters walk away from Jesus as changed people. Perhaps one of these dramatic encounters will enable the reader to find themselves and God's purpose in his or her own life. As the characters in John's gospel as well as myself, were impacted by our encounters with the Savior, so too will the readers of this book.

CHAPTER 1

Come, and ye shall see.

John opens his gospel by declaring the true identity of Jesus as the Christ. He deliberately takes his readers back to Genesis with the statement,

> **"In the beginning**... was the Word, and the Word was with God, and the Word was God. The same was in the beginning with God. All things were made through him; and without him was not anything made that hath been made. **(Joh 1:1-3)"** .... **vs,10-11** He was in the world, and the world was made by him, and the world knew him not. He came unto his own, and his own received him not. .... **vs.14** And the Word became flesh, and dwelt among us (and we beheld his glory, glory as of the only begotten from the Father), full of grace and truth.

John clearly wanted to present Jesus of Nazareth as Yahweh in the flesh. As he makes his introduction to the audience (readers of the gospel) with a lesson in theology or more specifically, Christology (the study of the person and work of Christ), he continues; **"He came unto his own, and they that were his own received him not. But as many as received him, to them gave he the right to become children of God, *even* to them that believe on his name: who were born, not of blood, nor of the will of the flesh, nor of the will of man, but of God."**

The first dramatic encounter recorded by the Apostle John is made with John the Baptizer, a distant cousin of the Lord. John's Mother Elizabeth carried him during the pregnancy of Jesus' mother Mary. His birth took place about four months prior to the birth of Jesus. The

Apostle bears witness to John as the forerunner of Messiah preparing the way.

> John beareth witness of him, and crieth, saying, This was he of whom I said, He that cometh after me is become before me: for he was before me. For of his fulness we all received, and grace for grace. For the law was given through Moses; grace and truth came through Jesus Christ. No man hath seen God at any time; the only begotten Son, who is in the bosom of the Father, he hath declared *him*. And this is the witness of John, when the Jews sent unto him from Jerusalem priests and Levites to ask him, Who art thou? (Joh 1:15-19)

As John the Baptizer was speaking to his disciples, "**behold, the lamb of God, who takes away the sin of the world.**" We witness the first dramatic encounter. To say that John truly understood his purpose would be an understatement. His preaching and baptizing in the wilderness had drawn great crowds. It also drew the attention of the Pharisees. These were a group of super religious Jews that controlled the religious and social life of the people. They prided themselves with their piety and religiosity. They had a form of godliness which was quite impressive, but completely devoid of any relationship with the God they supposedly worshiped or the people they proposed to minister to. John's ministry in the wilderness was so successful that even the Pharisees were curious about him. John completely shunned the religious trappings they were so accustomed to, preaching a doctrine of holiness and repentance not unlike that of their own, the Pharisees wondered, "who is this itinerate preacher?"

> And this is the record of John, when the Jews sent priests and Levites from Jerusalem to ask him, Who art thou? And he confessed, and denied not; but confessed, I am not the Christ. And they asked him, What then? Art thou Elias? And he saith, I am not. Art thou that prophet? And he answered, No. Then said they unto him, Who art thou? that we may give an answer to them that sent us. What sayest thou of thyself? (Joh 1:19-22)

The religious establishment, consisting of the Pharisees, the priests, Levites, and scribes had a monopoly on the socio-economic life of Israel. Although they were under Roman rule, it was the practice of Rome to allow their conquered territories a limited amount of autonomy and self rule. As long as the locals behaved themselves and submitted to the final authority of Caesar, they were allowed to control much of their own destiny. Rome was more interested in their tribute money than controlling every aspect of people's lives. Under this system, the establishment in Israel could not allow too much controversy, because it would cause Rome to intervene into their affairs. All of Israel was aware of the prophecies concerning the Messiah. Their hope was that Messiah would come and bring an end to the Roman rule. John was a herald declaring the coming of Messiah.

> He said, I *am* the voice of one crying in the wilderness, Make straight the way of the Lord, as said the prophet Esaias. And they which were sent were of the Pharisees. And they asked him, and said unto him, Why baptizest thou then, if thou be not that Christ, nor Elias, neither that prophet? John answered them, saying, I baptize with water: but there standeth one among you, whom ye know not; (Joh 1:23-26)

The Baptist had set the stage for the first dramatic encounter recorded by the Apostle. Downplaying his own encounter with the scribes, his retort, **"He it is, who coming after me is preferred before me, whose shoe's latchet I am not worthy to unloose."** Unlike any scribe or Pharisee, who would never in a million years defer religious importance to another nor ascribe to another preacher or teacher more eminence than themselves. John was not a part of the religious establishment and was not concerned about making a name or reputation for himself. His only ambition was to make way for the coming of the Lord. As he awaited Messiah, he continued with his ministry baptizing in Jordan and preaching repentance. When the dramatic day occurred, John was busy carrying out his mission, which brings us to the next significant controversy.

3

> The next day John seeth Jesus coming unto him, and saith, Behold the Lamb of God, which taketh away the sin of the world. This is he of whom I said, After me cometh a man which is preferred before me: for he was before me. And I knew him not: but that he should be made manifest to Israel, therefore am I come baptizing with water. And John bare record, saying, I saw the Spirit descending from heaven like a dove, and it abode upon him. And I knew him not: but he that sent me to baptize with water, the same said unto me, Upon whom thou shalt see the Spirit descending, and remaining on him, the same is he which baptizeth with the Holy Ghost. And I saw, and bare record that this is the Son of God. (Joh 1:29-34)

Behold..........the Lamb of God

On that day, countless individuals came to John, submitting to his baptism. He continued to preach the doctrine of repentance and the coming kingdom without any controversy until the next dramatic encounter occurred. Having received revelation knowledge by God the Father, that one whom he would baptize was indeed the Christ. He would know him by the sign of the dove descending like a spirit and remaining on him. Normally, doves would avoid humans but this was no ordinary dove, as the one he landed upon was no ordinary man. Once the baptism of Christ was complete, and the heavens opened up declaring God's pleasure in Him, John made no special mention of Him. Perhaps the audience was of a mixed multitude and not worthy of the revelation, but on the next day, in the presence of his own disciples, John made the dramatic declaration, "**Behold the Lamb of God,.......**". Why John would make the declaration while Jesus was afar off and not at hand is a mystery. Perhaps it was his intention to keep at a distance so his disciples would have to make a more volitional decision to retreat from him and follow Jesus. As John would later say, "He must increase, that I might decrease." To direct all attention to another preacher is something very few if any, twenty first century pastors or evangelists would ever dream of, let alone do.

One of John's disciples was a man named Andrew, whose dramatic encounter was so profound, it changed not only his own life, but the course of history.

> And the two disciples heard him speak, and they followed Jesus.
> Then Jesus turned, and saw them following, and saith unto
> them, What seek ye? They said unto him, Rabbi, (which is to
> say, being interpreted, Master,) where dwellest thou? He saith
> unto them, Come and see. They came and saw where he dwelt,
> and abode with him that day: for it was about the tenth hour.
> One of the two which heard John *speak*, and followed him, was
> Andrew, Simon Peter's brother. He first findeth his own brother
> Simon, and saith unto him, We have found the Messias, which
> is, being interpreted, the Christ.
> (Joh 1:37-41)

John the Apostle and Andrew were together on that day when they
met Jesus for the first time. They were so enamored by his presence
that they spent the entire afternoon with him. Jesus had made such
an impression, Andrew's response was not unlike a beggar who finds
free bread, he runs and tells his best beggar friend. In this case, the one
person in the world who was most dear to Andrew, was his elder brother
Simon. Faith comes by hearing the word of God and Andrew's faith in
Christ prompted him to share the good news of Messiah with the most
important person in his life. Not much is recorded of the life of Andrew.
It appears his purpose in life was to introduce to Jesus the one person
who would be used most mightily by him. He is mentioned only one
more time in the New Testament, at the feeding of the five thousand
(John 6:9); where he found the Lad who shares his lunch with the Savior.
Although the Savior uses another, Andrew is remembered for bringing
the key person at a key moment. If your posterity is to be bringing to
the Master someone who will be used to a greater degree than yourself,
it is a noble thing. Much like his first mentor John the Baptist, Andrew
probably gained much pleasure in knowing that it was not about himself,
it was about linking the hearts and minds of men to Jesus. The spirit
of Andrew lives on to inspire the saints through successive generations.
There have been many servants of God who would be considered giants,
men such as Charles and John Wesley, Charles Spurgeon, or Charles
Finney to name a few. But those men would never be known unless
someone such as an Edward Kimball would come alone in total obscurity
to share Jesus with a lost soul as he did with a young Dwight L. Moody,
who became one of the most renowned preachers, teacher, and evangelist

the world has ever known. Once you have a dramatic encounter with Jesus, and give yourself totally to him, the very fabric of your life is transformed to the point where nothing else matters but getting others to meet Jesus for themselves, so that they too, can be completely transformed by his grace.

Ever so often a holiday such as Christmas falls on Sunday. During one such year when Christmas Eve landed on a Saturday, Eternal Life Christian Fellowship, a ministry founded by my wife and I, decided to feed the homeless immediately after service on this particular day. It was a small church with limited resources, but we believed doing this type of outreach would be appreciated by the community and the young people in the congregation would have a good experience serving the needs of others. This particular neighborhood was known for its homelessness, public drunkenness, drugs, prostitution and low level street crimes common to inner cities. The First Lady and I, as well as the rest of the small congregation contributed and prepared most of the items for this feast. Mamas Nem's, a local soul food restaurant, over prepped turkey the night before and donated two large pans of roasted turkey wings to the feast. I was totally surprised by this unexpected blessing. The church did not have a dining room, so we took large tables and placed them in the parking lot and set up a buffet line. Using portable chafing dishes and warmers; the spread looked very impressive. Any food service professional would have been impressed. The delicious food was beautifully prepared and displayed and everything was all set to go. Once the children were fed, they donned aprons and serving gloves and made ready for the crowd, which to my dismay of never came. I wondered if maybe we had goofed preparing so much food. I dreaded being stuck with so many leftovers. One of the children boldly approached an obviously hungry homeless man and asked him if he wanted something to eat. The gentleman approached the youngster and replied, "yes, but I have no money." "You don't need any money, it's all free", replied the gregarious teen. "Is that why no one is coming, they think we are selling food on a holiday?" The homeless man retorted, "the other churches around here sell dinners or just feed themselves, hardly ever think about us." One of the teens was assigned the duty of manning the wash basin, allowing the people off the street to wash, dry and sanitize their hands. So the man washed up and got in line. Still no one else would come. So one of the other teens approached another passerby and asked if he wanted to eat with them. Looking at the first guy enjoying his holiday meal, he also washed up, got in line and got a styrofoam hinged plate. They were all fixed to go because there was no real seating available. The thirty or so folding chairs used for worship service, were removed from the Parramore Avenue storefront and arrayed in the parking lot for the enjoyment of whoever wanted to sit down and eat. The second man however, took the plate with him and walked around the corner and after a few minutes, people were lined up across the parking lot. I wondered where all those people suddenly came from. As it turned out, the second visitor went and told his friends about the food being given away around the corner. Suddenly, the entire neighborhood had thronged the little storefront church. Before long over two hundred people were fed that day. My wife and I had to eat at McDonalds, because all of the food was given out to the visitors. We were glad so many people were blessed by the meal and the opportunity to share the love and message of Jesus Christ. I did not care that we had to eat fast food while the others feasted. My meat was to do the will of him that sent me. That second visitor did what is typical of most men, when they have an encounter with Jesus, they run and tell other men what great things the Lord had done for them. In the words of Pastor Steve Brown of Reformed Theological Seminary, "the beggars always tell other beggars where to find bread."

CHAPTER 2

Whatsoever he saith unto you, do *it*.

And the third day there was a marriage in Cana of Galilee; and the mother of Jesus was there: And both Jesus was called, and his disciples, to the marriage. And when they wanted wine, the mother of Jesus saith unto him, They have no wine. Jesus saith unto her, Woman, what have I to do with thee? mine hour is not yet come. His mother saith unto the servants, Whatsoever he saith unto you, do *it*.   (**Joh 2:1-5**)

The next significant encounter with Jesus occurs at of all places, a wedding. What made the event significant was the fact that Mary, **the mother of Jesus was there**, along with his family and disciples. Apparently, Mary was a prominent person at this affair, possibly responsible for planning or procuring the necessities. In the orient, it was not uncommon for the wedding celebration to last several days, the more prominent the family, the longer the celebration. It was not atypical for the wedding festivities with family and friends to last a whole week, according to (Judges 14:17) the days of the marriage was said to be" thirty". This encounter set up a dilemma for Mary. They had run out of wine. It was an embarrassment of monumental proportions for the governor of the feast to run out of wine. Celebration and mirth was the order of the day, in this case week, and to run out wine would have created a laughingstock. With her back against the wall she went to the only person who could remedy the situation.

The wedding at Cana brings several important points to mind, first of all, in life, there will always be circumstances where the reason to celebrate will be lost. Calamity will come into our lives sooner or later.

When calamity does show its ugly head, it is important that someone in the midst knows Jesus. In the text, calamity manifested itself with the running out of wine, but in our day, calamity may take the form of extended unemployment, a negative doctor's report, or it may present itself as a foreclosure on your home. However calamity comes upon anyone, there will be no reason to celebrate. It will be as it was on that day in Cana of Galilee when the wine ran out and when it does, someone better know Jesus. The wedding also provided the reader with a reminder that it is important to look to the Word of God when faced with any crisis and act upon that Word with faith. It also showed that God has strategically and providentially provided the resources necessary for managing any crisis.

Up until this wedding at Cana, Jesus had done no public ministry or miraculous manifestations. The messianic clock had not been wound, but once he started, there would be no turning back. When his mother approached Him with the problem, his response appeared harsh in the translation. **"What have I to do with thee?"** The Greek literally says, "what to me and to thee?" Essentially, Jesus is saying to his mother, "do you know what you are asking"?..... "My time is not yet come." This dramatic encounter initiated the countdown to the cross. Knowing her son would never let her down, she immediately drew her attention to the servants with the order, "Whatsover he saith unto you, **do it.**" Not knowing what he would say, or what he would do, being the only person on earth knowing his true identity, Mary's confidence in her son was reflected in the resoluteness of her voice. His order, though illogical was followed to the amazement of the servants.

> **Jesus saith unto them, Fill the waterpots with water. And they filled them up to the brim. And he saith unto them, Draw out now, and bear unto the governor of the feast. And they bare *it.* When the ruler of the feast had tasted the water that was made wine, and knew not whence it was: (but the servants which drew the water knew;) the governor of the feast called the bridegroom, (Joh 2:7-9)**

After the water was poured into the waterpots, the servants were instructed to draw out the contents of the waterpots, in other words, to draw upon the resources at hand. Resources that had been assembled on the basis of and upon the commandment of the Word of God, whose contents were subject to, exposed to and submitted to God's anointing and Anointed one. Earle wrote, concerning the waterpots, "We believe that the filling of the water jars showed the completion of Judaism with its ceremonial cleansings. The unlimited supply of water from the well, turned into wine, symbolized the beginning of Christianity with its endless, joyful supply of God's grace."

The water was made wine. Not the cheap stuff, but the best wine. It is here that the governor of the feast reveals the best example for the posterity of all believers. When he tasted the wine, never knowing that a crisis had miraculously been averted, he called to celebrate the bridegroom. The bridegroom in this narrative is a type or metaphor of Jesus. In celebrating the bridegroom (lifting up Jesus), he was exalting the miraculous power of God. The servants and the disciples bear witness to the event. They heard the words of Jesus, acted in obedience and were rewarded with a manifestation of the glory of God which had never before been seen and would forever alter their destinies.

This beginning of miracles did Jesus in Cana of Galilee, and manifested forth his glory; and his disciples believed on him. (Joh 2:11)

Their obedience was rewarded with a faith that would carry them the rest of their days. Jesus was now poised to carry out His Father's business. Those disciples whom he had called, and who were with him at this marriage, and were made acquainted with this miracle: and though they believed in him before, and had declared, and professed him to be the Messiah that Moses and the prophets spoke of, and the Son of God, and King of Israel, yet by this miracle they were, more and more convinced of these things. In addition, others including the wedding servants most likely became his disciples at this time, as they were also led to believe on him. This would be the pattern that every disciple who would come to him should follow. Whatever he tells you to do, do it without question, do it without hesitation and you will be rewarded with a manifestation of his glory.

I was reminded by this narrative of my own call into the Gospel Ministry. While still serving as a Deacon in my local church, I recalled a bible study lesson conducted for a young men's ministry, dealing with 'honoring your parents'. While preparing for the lesson, the Holy Spirit brought to my mind a passage of scripture from 1 Timothy chapter 5, dealing with widows. The Holy Spirit reminded me that by caring for my widowed aunt, I was also by this deed, honoring my own mother. While contemplating this biblical truth, I saw in a vision himself and many of my cousins all painting our aunts house. It was an old house built by Jim Walter Homes some thirty years earlier, which was badly in need of a new coat of paint. Interpreting this vision as a commandment from God to honor my own mother by painting her sister's house, stirred me to action. My aunt had scores of grandchildren, mostly girls, but an abundance of able bodied nephews. So I, contacted my brothers and cousins, all who appeared in the vision and told them of the dream of all of us painting our aunts house. I appealed to them to come together and make it happen. Many of them agreed to help with the painting, some agreed to help purchase the paint. With collective action, the cost per man would be minimal and the smile on Aunt's face would be priceless. After some coaxing and planning, the nephews got together and made a day of it including a barbeque. After some hours, the task was accomplished and the aging aunt was never happier. The sight of her nephews painting and working together, blessed her immensely and was a moment that she would never forget, neither would we. The greatest lesson, however, occurred after all the painting was done and the group of nephews were all sitting down fellowshipping together and eating barbeque.

It was then; I looked onto a field straddling the property line of my aunt and our late grandparents. I had noticed some green sour sprouts, less than a foot tall extruding out of the ground. There were no citrus trees there, only oak clusters and weeds which seemed odd to me. At that point, my asked his Cousin Ben, who was named after our grandfather, "where did those sour sprouts come from?" "There are no orange trees in this area." Ben replied, "don't you remember, that's where Papa Ben had his citrus nursery many years ago, those roots never died." It was at that point, when the vision came. It was as if heaven opened up and a sheet fell from heaven like a projector screen, showing myself in a fallow field, hoeing out weeds. In the vision, the field was as far as the eye could see with me hoeing out the weeds. As I cleared a small area, the voice instructed me to sow the seeds which sort of appeared in a small bag. The amount of seed was not nearly enough to sow in the prepared area, but I obeyed the voice anyway. The voice from heaven said, "keep digging out the weeds, something will grow and someone else will come alongside to sow, otherwise when this harvest comes in,you can sow where you have tilled." The hoeing of weeds represented the teaching ministry of the Pastor, the sowing of seed represented the ministry of evangelism. It was in the vision, that the I knew that the Deacon's ministry was not God's call for me, but the Gospel ministry. At that moment, I extended my hand to the gospel plow, never to let it go. Within months, I was enrolled in Seminary and began the formal preparation of my life's calling. The elevation was revealed following my obedience to the first vision, the first command to honor my mother by serving her elder sister. As the servants of the wedding feast obeyed the direct command of Jesus and were rewarded with privilege of witnessing a manifestation of his glory, and I, as a co-laborer, was also rewarded as a participant in the manifestations of Christ's glory.

❖ I Don't Think So

Shortly thereafter, there was another encounter with Jesus, not much unlike that of the wedding. It was during the Jewish Passover, which brought him to the temple. This event like the wedding brought a lot of people together for a festive though serious occasion. Passover had elements of mirth as well as the sacred components just as the wedding, but it was about to produce something the wedding did not.

> And the Jews' passover was at hand, and Jesus went up to Jerusalem, And found in the temple those that sold oxen and sheep and doves, and the changers of money sitting: And when he had made a scourge of small cords, he drove them all out of the temple, and the sheep, and the oxen; and poured out the changers' money, and overthrew the tables; And said unto them that sold doves, Take these things hence; make not my Father's house an house of merchandise. And his disciples remembered that it was written, The zeal of thine house hath eaten me up. Then answered the Jews and said unto him, What sign shewest thou unto us, seeing that thou doest these things? (Joh 2:13-18)

The scene at the temple brought out a quality in Jesus, the uninitiated might not have been prepared for. I recalled during my childhood, watching a film of the life of Jesus, THE GREATEST STORY EVER TOLD, and watching the scene taking place here. Having not the benefit of Sunday School training as a young child, and unaware of the story, I could not believe my eyes. Someone in the theater cried, "Jesus never did anything like that!" Obviously that person was also ignorant of biblical facts, as was I. Watching an actor portray Jesus, turning over tables and chasing men out of the temple with a whip, seemed blasphemous, yet the portrayal was historically accurate. In retrospect, the righteous indignation which seemed overly dramatic at the time, should have been the expected response from the Son of God coming home to see his Father's House defiled by thieves and hypocrites. The religious people running the temple, the priests, Levites, scribes, and Pharisees had an agenda which was contrary to that of the one whom they purported to serve. Jesus was having no part of their hypocrisy and would not let their vulgarism and defilement stand. The visit to the temple should have produced mirth and joy, as did the wedding but it did not. Since the hearts of the Jews in the temple were hardened, and their eyes were darkened by greed and their ears spiritually deaf, they could not experience the presence of God, nor recognize His anointed, nor hear His voice. As impressive as they were in their outward appearance, their worship was devoid of the love and praise which moves the heart of God. In his book, *JUSTICE-God, Nations, and Systems*, **Dr. Glover** described the temple system appropriately, "For the priests, the temple was not about worship, but financial markets. It was not people, but about profits; not about securing favor with God, but protecting the status quo with Caesar. If the love of money is the root of all evil, then the root cause of the corruption, extortion, exploitation, and fraud in the temple worship system was the priest's love for profit and power." It was at this point, that the religious establishment began to plot his destruction. In order for scripture to be fulfilled, it was only proper and fitting that this would be their response. The stage was set for the next dramatic encounter **in Jerusalem at the Passover, in the feast *day*, many believed in his name, when they saw the miracles which he did.**

13

CHAPTER 3

.......except God be with him.

> There was a man of the Pharisees, named Nicodemus, a ruler of the Jews:
> The same came to Jesus by night, and said unto him, Rabbi, we know that
> thou art a teacher come from God: for no man can do these miracles that
> thou doest, except God be with him. Jesus answered and said unto him,
> Verily, verily, I say unto thee, Except a man be born again, he cannot see the
> kingdom of God. Nicodemus saith unto him, How can a man be born when
> he is old? can he enter the second time into his mother's womb, and be born?
> **(Joh 3:1-4)**

Neutrality is not an option after an encounter with Jesus. He would
not allow anyone to remain unmoved. You will either be drawn to him
or repulsed by him. You will either love him or conspire to his demise,
but one will never be indifferent to him. Following the commotion at
the temple and subsequent actions, a chain of events transpired that
changed the landscape surrounding Jerusalem and Judea. What began
in Cana of Galilee was followed up in the vicinity of Jerusalem, by other
miracles and manifestations of the power of God. Jesus' fame spread
quickly. There was no Twitter, Facebook, or cell-phones, yet the news
spread just as quickly. Every corner of society had heard of Him. The
Pharisees were seriously disturbed by his presence and sought to put an
end to this doctrine. His teachings, though not much different from their
own, excited the people and created a buzz in the atmosphere. Suddenly,
the influence of the Pharisees over the minds of the people was challenged
and they would share their glory with no one, not even God nor His
Anointed. Upon seeing the miracles at the temple, many believed on him.

Perhaps among the witnesses was a Pharisee named Nicodemus. It had been speculated that Nicodemus was sent by the Sanhedrin to recruit him to their cause. Unlike his colleagues however, who encountered Jesus, he possibly listened to him speak or even witnessed his miracles, Nicodemus was probably drawn to him of his own curiosity. He was fascinated by this man. It did not matter to Nicodemus, where he learned his doctrine or with whom he associated. Jesus' words exposed within Nicodemus an emptiness that he was heretofore unaware of. It revealed within the recesses of his heart, an inadequacy previously unknown yet too powerful to ignore. When human wisdom is exposed to the wisdom of God, it pales in comparison and Nicodemus knew he had to get more. Being the politician that he was, Nicodemus felt that going directly to Jesus would have negative consequences amongst his peers and was not prepared to risk his professional reputation and status among the ruling elite. Nevertheless, his curiosity and compulsion got the best of him.

❖ In the Dead of Night

Like an adulterer coming to see his mistress, Nicodemus went to Jesus in the dead of night. I recalled a time some decades earlier, prior to my salvation, making clandestine moves to score (illicit drugs). Among the community of hustlers and dealers, discretion was out of order. It was common practice to campaign for street cred. However, in regards to law enforcement, it was necessary to be as evasive as possible. Detection by the cops meant going to jail, so discretion was the order of the day. Nicodemus' need for secrecy was completely understandable from a pragmatic point of view, especially if he had not been sent by the Sanhedrin. In his mind, the risk of detection and its consequences would have been as profoundly negative as the risks I had taken so many years earlier. In the old crime dramas, it was the dead of night that provided protection from discovery. The prostitute meets her john in the dead of night. The thief breaks and enters a home in the dead of night. The spy would execute his black bag job in the dead of night. Nicodemus, a pious Jew, would take his cue from those least like himself. The most dramatic encounter in all of scripture takes place in the dead of night.

What was most intriguing about the exchange was not so much the hour of the visit, but in how Nicodemus addressed Jesus. He calls him, **"Rabbi"** or "my master", a term of respect and authority. The name

Nicodemus means in Hebrew, 'victorious among his people', and he is identified as a Ruler in Jerusalem, one residing on the Sanhedrin Council. Yet he clearly takes a subservient position. From a human standpoint, it is Nicodemus who has the legitimate authority, but clearly he defers to Jesus. He gives the reason for his apparent humility in the next statement, **"we know that thou art a teacher come from God: for no man can do these miracles that thou doest, except God be with him."** It was unlikely at that point that Nicodemus recognized him to be the Messiah of Israel, but he surely knew that in Jesus of Nazareth, there was a power neither he nor any of his ilk possessed. Also apparent in this exchange, is a pattern which would be repeated throughout his ministry, Jesus always responded to the personal, core issue of those who sought and engaged him. Unlike his cohorts, Nicodemus was able to recognize that there was something lacking in Phariseeism. With all their religious trappings and shows of holiness, no Pharisee had ever performed a miracle. Nicodemus believed that Jesus was the real deal and conversely, that they, the Pharisees were the frauds. They ascribed the miracles performed by Jesus to the power of Beelzebub (the devil), but Nicodemus recognized the authentic power of God. But there was something else in Nicodemus that his colleagues also lacked; there was an authentic desire to know God. It was on that basis where Jesus ministered to him.

❖ You Must Be Born Again

> Jesus answered and said unto him, Verily, verily, I say unto thee, Except a man be born again, he cannot see the kingdom of God. (Joh 3:3)

The most profound statement ever uttered to man was given under cover of darkness to a man made aware of the tragedy of his own soul. It was the natural, pragmatic, logical, technical mind of Nicodemus that was failing him now. In the council, his reasoning served him well, but now. It was useless in discerning the deep things of God.

> Nicodemus saith unto him, How can a man be born when he is old? can he enter the second time into his mother's womb, and be born? (Joh 3:4)

Jesus goes on to teach the teacher about the new birth, the nature of man and the futility of external religion. Initially, Nicodemus is dumb to spiritual things, but as Jesus continues to explain, the light of truth goes on and he is able to see the kingdom for the first time. All men must allow the grace of God to illuminate the darkness of their hearts to receive anything from Him.

But he that doeth truth cometh to the light, that his deeds may be made manifest, that they are wrought in God. (Joh 3:21)

But he that doeth truth,.... That which is true, right and good: "he whose work is just", or, "he who performs with right motives", that which is according to the will of God, and from a principle of love to him, and with a view to his glory: **cometh to the light;** to Christ, and to his words, and ordinances: **that his deeds may be made manifest;** being brought to the light, as a test, and standard, whether they, are right, or wrong; and that it may appear, **that they are wrought in God;** or "by God"; by his empowerment, and gracious influence, without which men can do nothing; for it is God that works in them both to will and to do according to His good pleasure, both for matter and manner: for the glory of God, which ought to be the aim, and end of every action, that the work which is between God and him may be known; that such deeds may be discovered, which are only known to God and himself. This dramatic encounter between Christ and Nicodemus would affect how others, including myself, would approach our own view of the things of God.

Soon after the encounter with Nicodemus, another controversy occurred, but this time, Jesus was not there. It involved the remaining disciples of John, as he was winding down his ministry, still preaching, still baptizing, still fulfilling his mission. It was reported to John of the one whom he testified of (Jesus) was now preaching and baptizing and many people were now following him. The communication could be compared to a junkie coming to his regular supplier of dope, explaining that another dealer had a better package than himself and all the other junkies were now coming to him, or the news to a shop keeper of the opening up of a Super Walmart around the corner and all of his regular customers were now shopping at the Walmart. Unlike the dealer or the shop keeper, John's response showed no sign of anger, animosity or regret.

> John answered and said, A man can receive nothing, except it be given him
> from heaven. Ye yourselves bear me witness, that I said, I am not the Christ,
> but that I am sent before him. He that hath the bride is the bridegroom: but
> the friend of the bridegroom, which standeth and heareth him, rejoiceth
> greatly because of the bridegroom's voice: this my joy therefore is fulfilled.
> **(Joh 3:27-29)**

A man can receive nothing, "of his own will" and one needs to understand this of Christ, as man, who did not take upon him the character of the Messiah, nor the office of a Mediator, nor the honor of it of himself. He received the gifts and graces of the Spirit of God, without measure, and secured his success in his work from above; which can be said of both Christ, and John. As his messenger and forerunner, it was from Christ, John received his office, and honor, and all his gifts qualifying for it, and his success in it, not of himself, but of God: and since therefore the superior office, and honor, and usefulness of the one above the other, were according to the sovereign will of God, there was no room for complaint, murmuring, and envy; but there ought to be contentment and pleasure in the wise disposition of things by God. John clearly understood that those who came first to him and were now following Jesus were where they were supposed to be. So too was the disciple who brought the complaint. Every preacher of the gospel should remember, the disciples belong to Christ, not you. The only reason they should have come to you is because you were lifting up Jesus. **Except it be given him from heaven**; from God who dwells there, who is the author and donor of every gift, temporal, spiritual, and eternal. Especially those gifts man cannot perceive, nor discern, nor Gospel truths he could not receive, as it appeared to John his disciples could not. Unless spiritual light is given from above; and such a favor is bestowed, as to know the mysteries of the kingdom of heaven: and therefore, for every office, whether of a superior, or inferior kind, and for every degree of honor, and for whatsoever blessing and gift, whether for soul or body, for time, or for eternity, men ought to be thankful, and not glory in them, as though they had not received them; nor is there any reason to murmur against God, or envy one another, as these disciples did. As the doctrine of the Pharisees sustained Nicodemus as long as he did not know any better, so too the doctrine of John sustained his disciples. But once they would hear

Jesus, the inferiority of John's doctrine would be made known to them. And John was okay with that.

It is amazing of the plethora of bad and inadequate doctrine prevailing in the churches today. The people of God are either too lazy or too undiscerning to reject the false teachings or are otherwise complicit in it. Erroneous and at times heretical teachings have shipwrecked many men's souls. I recall attending a meeting where the speaker (can't call them preacher), was supposedly prophesying over the lives of some attendees, when it was time to bring the Word of God, the speaker never opened a bible and declared that God had already spoken during the prophesy. Many in the crowd were jumping and hollering all over the place, shouting Amen! Amen! Quite frankly, I was ready to walk out the door. I completely understood the sadness of Jesus when He cried over Jerusalem. For those Saints to be satisfied with preaching without the word was a travesty, but even more so for the Angel of that house to allow the mockery to go on. To profane the gospel message with vain and empty religious activity and pass it off as worship exposes the cross to an open shame.

CHAPTER 4

.....thou hast nothing to draw with

The circumstances of the next great encounter occurred in a circuitous manner. It appeared as if Jesus was attempting to deliberately slow the momentum of his ministry. From a contemporary ministry standpoint (or modern marketing for that matter), it is unusual for a preacher (or politician) to abandon a campaign where the crowds are rapidly growing and the word of mouth publicity machine is at a fever pitch. Nevertheless, this is exactly what Jesus did.

> When therefore the Lord knew how the Pharisees had heard that Jesus made and baptized more disciples than John, (Though Jesus himself baptized not, but his disciples,) He left Judaea, and departed again into Galilee. And he must needs go through Samaria. Then cometh he to a city of Samaria, which is called Sychar, near to the parcel of ground that Jacob gave to his son Joseph. **(Joh 4:1-5)**

Jesus, who is Lord of all, Lord of lords, the one and only Lord of saints, who knew all things as God. He knows every man, and what is in man; who would believe in him, and who not, and who would betray him. He knew his adversaries, what they thought, said, or did; what was told them, and how it operated in them. So the Pharisees, this hardened bunch of religious thugs, so determined to do him in and stop the spread of his (in their minds) cancerous doctrine, were no surprise to him. He knew what was in them. Although it may have appeared that Jesus was running from them, it was more likely that his intention was simply to slow the momentum and not allow events to get ahead of his plan. The decision to depart from Judea and go back to Galilee by way of Samaria surely must have caught his disciples by surprise. The route chosen surely had to be as big a shock as the timing. A comparison could be made to a modern circus leaving a metropolis such as Chicago in the springtime, with sold out performances and advance ticket sales for six weeks and heading to Fargo North Dakota, population 6300. From a marketing standpoint, it made no sense. Looking at it from a logistical point of view, it was a straight shot through Samaria. Other than some rough terrain, the distance was shorter than the usual route taken by the Jews, because they preferred to go by way of the Jordan river, adding some twenty five miles of distance to the journey. It was the cultural divide that made the trip so unlikely. The Jews had no dealings with the Samaritans. They looked upon them as unclean outcasts that needed to be avoided at all cost. They would rather wear out a donkey and go the extra miles if it would allow them to avoid a Samaritan city. On another occasion, Jesus forbade his disciples and to avoid the gentile cities, but this time, He had a divine appointment in Samaria.

> **Then cometh he to a city of Samaria, which is called Sychar, near to the parcel of ground that Jacob gave to his son Joseph. Now Jacob's well was there. Jesus therefore, being wearied with *his* journey, sat thus on the well: *and* it was about the sixth hour. (Joh 4:5-6)**

Jesus being wearied from his journey, travelling all day on foot was in need of rest by the time he approached this pivotal point. As significant as the place was in Jewish history, this was not the reason he was there. **Sychar,....** Now called Neapolis is the same as "Sichem", or "Shechem". More likely the new name was given to it by the time of Christ; and might be so called, either from, "Socher", which signifies a grave; because here, Joseph and the rest of the patriarchs were buried, <u>Jos 24:32</u>. Or rather, it was a name of reproach, and so called, from, "drunken"; since the Ephraimites, the descendents of Joseph, which dwelt in these parts, were infamous for the sin of drunkenness. A dramatic encounter had been ordained that had to come to pass. **There cometh a woman of Samaria,....** Or "out of Samaria"; not out of the city of Samaria, but out of the country of Samaria; out of Sychar, a city of Samaria and her coming was not by chance, but by the providence of God. This was not just any woman, but an infamous one with a bad reputation and self esteem issues. In Judea, Jesus had the opportunity to minister to hundreds, perhaps thousands, but this broken spirited woman was his chosen vessel that salvation was coming to and nothing could prevent it. **To draw water.......** for her normal use and service, she'd thought little of a meeting at Jacob's well. It was customary for the women to draw water for the days use early in the morning, before the heat of the sun would make even more difficult the carrying of a heavy water pot. By the time Jesus had arrived at high noon, all the women had long completed this task and returned to their homes. On this particular day however, it was different. In her mind, this woman chose to come at noon knowing she would be able to avoid the other women. She was tired of their ridicule, their snide comments, even their outright hostilities. Having known (in the biblical sense) many of the other women's husbands, this woman wanted only to get her water in peace and not have to put up with the "other woman" drama. This was obviously a woman who felt deeply but was resigned to the idea that her life would never be fulfilling and circumstances were beyond her control. She probably felt like many broken women who have been used by men. In order to survive, she has to use them back. She probably felt that self pride would not pay the bills or get groceries into the house and the scorching heat of the sun was no more uncomfortable than the sweaty stench of the men who lusted after and used her for their own pleasures. Of the many encounters she has had with men, this one began like many others, with a man asking something of her. **Jesus saith unto her, "give me to drink"** that is, water to drink, out of the pot or pitcher, she brought with her, for he was thirsty. **Then saith the woman of Samaria unto him,....** with a hint of sarcasm, **"how is it, that thou being a Jew;"** which she might know, by his language and his dress, **"askest drink of me, which am a woman of Samaria?"** Just as the high noon water run, the sarcasm in her voice was also a defense mechanism. But Jesus knowing what was in man, was not at all moved by her comment. So accustomed was this woman to harsh treatment from Jews to her and her kind, she expected more of the same, the same religious bigotry, the same religious snobbery. She was totally taken aback by his response. **Jesus answered and said unto her,....** In a very serious manner, in a different tone and manner from hers: **"if thou knewest the gift of God"**, meaning, not the Holy Spirit with his charismatic gifts and graces, as some think, but of himself, as the following explains, "**and who it is that saith to thee, give me to drink.**" Christ was often spoken of as a gift to mankind from God (eg. Isa 9:6, Jn 3:16) and surely this was his purpose here. He is his own and only begotten Son, and he is given for a covenant to the people, with all the promises and blessings of it; and as the head, both of eminence and influence; and to be a Savior of them, and a sacrifice for their sins; and as the bread of life, for them to feed and live upon; of which gift, men are naturally ignorant, as this woman was. He had no form, nor comeliness; and when we shall see him, *there is* no beauty that we should desire him. Yet here he was speaking life and hope into the spirit of a woman, who did not believe it was possible. Every word spoken by Jesus to this woman was exposing the issues of life. Pain, doubt, guilt, every hidden negative emotion was bubbling to the surface of her mind. "**thou wouldst have asked of him**"; an act of kindness and benefit; for such who truly know Christ, the worth and value of him, and their need of him, will apply to him for grace, as they have opportunity to do. **And he would have given thee living water.** The spiritual dearth of this woman was never more apparent than at the moment she replied.

> **The woman saith unto him, Sir, thou hast nothing to draw with, and the well is deep: from whence then hast thou that living water? Art thou greater than our father Jacob, which gave us the well, and drank thereof himself, and his children, and his cattle? Jesus answered and said unto her, Whosoever drinketh of this water shall thirst again: (Joh 4:11-13)**

Jesus was speaking of spiritual things, but she could only apprehend the carnal, natural things. But the natural man receiveth not the things of the Spirit of God: for they are foolishness unto him: neither can he know *them*, because they are spiritually discerned. Discernment is the tool by which spiritual insight is drawn. The Samaritan woman was correct in her self assessment. She had nothing to draw with. The depth of the rich resources of God is unfathomable. The organ of understanding of the deep things of God is not the human brain, which this woman and all natural men are apt to use, but the mind of God. But faith in God, comes by hearing the Word of God, who in the flesh was speaking to her. Whether she knew it or not, she was on the verge of a major spiritual upgrade. Whether her remark was in a mocking manner or sheer ignorance, one could not know, but it was obvious she lacked the tools necessary for communicating truth from God. This exchange initiated a spiritual trigger however, because the woman evoked the name of Jacob into the conversation, thinking a Jew would be impressed by that. This could be compared to an unbeliever mentioning church attendance in a conversation with devout believers giving testimony of their own salvation experiences. The unbeliever sees no difference between the two, and does not see the futility of empty religious expression. Just as Nicodemus became aware of the futility of religious ceremony without a relationship with the object of one's worship, this Samaritan woman too would come to realize the futility of religious experience without true knowledge of one being worshipped.

❖ Getting To The Point

> But whosoever drinketh of the water that I shall give him shall never thirst; but the water that I shall give him shall be in him a well of water springing up into everlasting life. The woman saith unto him, Sir, give me this water, that I thirst not, neither come hither to draw. Jesus saith unto her, Go, call thy husband, and come hither. (Joh 4:14-16)

Although the woman does not fully understand, she is becoming more aware of the spiritual references made by Jesus. She realizes that the water Jesus refers to is something greater than the water of Jacob's well. She also decides to ask for it. But she still thinks in the natural. Jesus needs to probe further into her soul to reveal to her the true problem. **Jesus saith unto her,.....** Observing that she continued as an ignorant scoffer at him, and his words, determined to take another method with her; and convince her, that he was not a common and ordinary person she was conversing with, as she took him to be; and also what a sinner she was, and what a wretched lifestyle she had lived; so that she might see that she stood in need of him, as the gift of God, and Savior of men; and of the grace he had been speaking of, under the notion of living water: saying to her, "**go, call thy husband, and come hither,**" go directly to the city of Sychar, and call thy husband, and come back with him. Christ said this, not to have him come and receive instruction himself, nor that he might be with her, a partaker of the same grace; but to bring on some further conversation, by which she would understand that he knew her state and condition, and what a course of life she now lived, and so bring her under a conviction of her sin and danger, and need of him and his grace.

❖ The Truth That Sets Men Free

> The woman answered and said, I have no husband. Jesus said unto her, Thou hast well said, I have no husband: For thou hast had five husbands; and he whom thou now hast is not thy husband: in that saidst thou truly. The woman saith unto him, Sir, I perceive that thou art a prophet. **(Joh 4:17-19)**

The woman's acknowledgement that she had no husband would not have been made to any other person, or any other time. Since she saw no reason to embellish her piety (what little she had) nor to shade her wretchedness (which was in abundance), she simply spoke the truth to this stranger, who couldn't possibly know otherwise. But Jesus, God in the flesh, who knows all things, delivers the truth that sets men free."**For thou hast had five husbands**",.... Which she either had been lawfully married, and either divorced (the Jews perfected low fault divorce) or had buried one after another; and which was no crime. The Sadducees posed a scenario to Jesus where a woman had had seven husbands, and who of the seven would be her husband in heaven, though the Sadducee believed neither in heaven nor the resurrection. It is amazing how often the cults know the truth yet choose to cling to lies. "**And he whom thou now hast, is not thy husband.**" The anonymity she comforted herself with engaging this strange Jew was now stripped of her. "How could he know these things about me, accept the Lord be with him?", mused the woman. **The woman saith unto him, "Sir,**.... With another expression, and a different air and gesture, with another accent and tone of speech, dropping her scoffs and jeers: **I perceive ....that thou art a prophet.**" Like unto Samuel was, who could tell Saul what was in his heart, and that his father's asses were found, and where they were, **1Sa_9:19**; and as Elisha, whose heart went with his servant Gehazi, when Naaman turned to him to meet him, and give him presents; and who could tell, before the king's messenger came to him, that the son of a murderer had sent to take away his head, **2Ki_5:26**. And such a prophet, that had such a spirit of discerning, this woman took Christ to be; and who indeed is more than a prophet. The sarcasm was quickly replaced with false piety and a quick change to churchspeak. Churchspeak is the religious jargon used by nominal Christians to appear to be genuine believers. They know when to clap, shout and say "praise the Lord", but their hearts are far from him. **"Our fathers worshipped in this mountain"**,.... Mount Gerizim, which was just by, and within sight; so that the woman could point to it. By the "fathers", this woman claims as theirs, are meant, not the immediate ancestors of the Samaritans, or those only of some few generations past; but the patriarchs Abraham, Isaac, and Jacob. She implies a history of worship experience in the very spot. According to the historian Josephus, their tradition suggests such an experience, but as for any temple, or place of worship on this mount, there was none till of late years, even after the second temple was built. Any attempt to hide behind a veneer of religious worship was about to be stripped off. **"And ye say, that in Jerusalem is the place where men ought *to* worship"**, that is, in the temple at Jerusalem; who correctly urged that God had chosen that place to put his name, and establish his worship there; and had ordered them to come, and bring their offerings and sacrifices, and to keep their Passover and other feasts. For the woman to compare the polluted rituals of Mt. Gerizim to the orthodoxy of Jerusalem was almost pathetic, but Jesus knew that within her was a true desire to know God. She lived in an environment where a true knowledge of God was not possible.

> Jesus saith unto her, Woman, believe me, the hour cometh, when ye shall neither in this mountain, nor yet at Jerusalem, worship the Father. Ye worship ye know not what: we know what we worship: for salvation is of the Jews. But the hour cometh, and now is, when the true worshippers shall worship the Father in spirit and in truth: for the Father seeketh such to worship him. God *is* a Spirit: and they that worship him must worship *him* in spirit and in truth.   **(Joh 4:21-24)**

Worship is not about a place, but a personal knowledge and relationship with the one who is worshiped. God is a spirit, and not a body, or a physical substance. The nature and essence of God is like a spirit, simple and uncompounded, not made up of parts, nor is it divisible, nor does it admit of any change and alteration. God, as a spirit, is immaterial, immortal, invisible, and an intelligent, willing, and active being; but differs from other spirits, in that he is not created, but an immense and infinite spirit, and an eternal one, which has neither beginning nor end: he is therefore a spirit by way of eminency, as well as effectively, he being the author and former of all spirits: whatever excellence is in them, must be ascribed to God in the highest manner; and whatever is imperfect in them, must be removed from him: **And they that worship him**; worship is due to him on account of his nature and perfections, both internal and external; with both the bodies and souls of men; and both private and public; in the closet, in the family, and in the church of God; as prayer, praise, attendance on the word and ordinances.

Once Jesus expounded on the doctrine of worship, the woman was finally able to see the futility of vain worship and recognize the depravity of her soul. She was able to communicate a truth hidden within the recesses of her heart, the longing of Messiah. When sin consumes the psyche of a man (or woman), truths previously known become obscured. Whatever morality one may have had, becomes lost. The ability to receive a revelation of God or from God is also lost. It is only until God draws us out and speaks to us through the haze of our sinful existence will we realize our need for Him. **I know that Messias cometh which is called Christ**: the last clause, "which is called Christ" is not the words of the woman, but that of the evangelist. The knowledge of the coming of the Messiah was not atypical to this woman, but was common to all the Samaritans, as they received the five books of Moses and had some history with the scriptures, although much of this had been lost to the woman. ....**when he is come he will tell us all things**; the whole mind and will of God; all things relating to the worship of God, and to the salvation of men. (writers words, not hers) Faith (the ability to believe and act upon) comes by hearing the word of God. By His revealing her to herself, was she brought up from her sunken condition to a frame of mind and heart capable of apprehending the things of God.

Uncharacteristic of Jesus, He gives to this Samaritan woman something that he withheld from his own people. **I that speak unto thee am *he***; This is a wonderful instance of the grace of Christ to this woman, that he should make himself known in such a non cryptic manner, to so simple a person, and so wretched a creature as she had been: we never find

27

that he ever made so clear a revelation of himself, in such express terms, to any, as to her, unless it were to his immediate disciples; and these he would sometimes charge not to tell who he was. After receiving this revelatory gift, she is interrupted by the arrival of the disciples, who had gone into Sychar to buy meat.

> And upon this came his disciples, and marvelled that he talked with the woman: yet no man said, What seekest thou? or, Why talkest thou with her? The woman then left her waterpot, and went her way into the city, and saith to the men, Come, see a man, which told me all things that ever I did: is not this the Christ? (Joh 4:27-29)

Strangely, the disciples came onto the scene without comment. It must have appeared unusual to them that Jesus would have an extended conversation with a strange woman, let alone, a Samaritan. According to Dr. Earle, the Jewish rule states, "it was never appropriate for a man to converse with a woman in public, not even his own wife, sister, or mother." Nevertheless, they remained silent and kept all questions and objections to themselves. The disciples possibly even remembered their own states when they came into fellowship with Jesus, compelled them to remain quiet, even Peter. Notwithstanding, the woman's response to the revelation was typical of one who has a dramatic encounter with Jesus. **The woman then left her water pot,**.... Most likely an earthen vessel she brought with her to the well to draw water in. She had a total shift in priorities. Her reason for coming to the well was to receive the natural water, but her reason for leaving was to carry the living water (which required no waterpot). **And went her way into the city** of Sychar, to inform her friends, relations, and neighbors what she had met the Messiah. As did Andrew and Philip, when they had found Christ for themselves went and told the others and brought them to him. So did Levi, the publican, being called himself by Christ, then makes a feast for Christ, and invites many if his publican and sinner friends to sit down with him, that they might know him as well as himself. ....**and saith to the men**; no doubt the men of the place in general are meant and not only those of her family, but the inhabitants of the city. It is interesting that she chose to reveal the good news to the men and not the women. It was the men who treated her more kindly, so her natural response was to take the message to those she felt more linked to. **Come, see a man,....** An exceptional, extraordinary man, a prophet, who himself says, he is the Messiah, who is now at Jacob's well; come and accompany me, and see him for yourselves. Judge for yourselves as to who, and what he is.

> Then they went out of the city, and came unto him. In the mean while his disciples prayed him, saying, Master, eat. But he said unto them, **I have meat to eat that ye know not of.** Therefore said the disciples one to another, Hath any man brought him *ought* to eat? Jesus saith unto them, **My meat is to do the will of him that sent me, and to finish his work.** (Joh 4:30-34)

❖ The Impact of a Good Witness

As the woman was gone out from among them and returned to the city, Jesus used the time with his disciples to expound on personal evangelism and witnessing for the Kingdom. The woman was busy carrying out the mission. She knew exactly where the target of evangelism was, back home. And she wasted no time doing just that. On the return trip, she indubitably magnified and lifted up Jesus to her audience. In spite of her reputation with the women of Sychar, the men found her easy to believe. Perhaps it was because of the transformation of her countenance, the zeal by which she spoke or some other reason, nevertheless she had some credibility with them and they came. **And many of the Samaritans of that city,... believed on him**; that he was truly the Messiah he had told the woman he was; and she queried them whether he was or not. Prior to seeing Him, or had any conversation with Him themselves, they believed, **for the saying of the woman which testified, he told me all that ever I did.** The account she gave was so plain, and honest, and disinterested, that she could not mess it up, and since the person was a total stranger to her, and yet had laid before her the panoply of her life story, they concluded he could be none other than the Messiah, who should tell all things, and was able to disclose the secrets of men.

> So when the Samaritans were come unto him, they besought him that he would tarry with them: and he abode there two days. And many more believed because of his own word; And said unto the woman, Now we believe, not because of thy

saying: for we have heard *him* ourselves, and know that this is indeed the Christ, the Saviour of the world. (Joh 4:40-42)

.....and many more believed because of his own word.......for we heard him ourselves.

❖ At The Same Hour

Shortly after the encounters in Samaria, Jesus returned to Galilee by way of Cana only to find curiosity seekers. Many of the Galileans were present at the feasts in Jerusalem and were aware of the miracles he performed there and wanted to see the same. Their interest in him had probably become an annoyance because it appeared they were more interested in what he could do rather than the message he preached. **For Jesus himself testified, "that a prophet hath no honour in his own country."** He was not treated with the same disrespect he suffered in his home town Nazareth, but their treatment of him paled in comparison to the Samaritans of Sychar. Suddenly, there appeared a certain nobleman whose son was terminally ill seeking Jesus' assistance. The nobleman was from Capernaum, about a days journey from Cana, on the northern shore of Sea of Galilee. This man had heard of Jesus and his prior exploits at the wedding, turning water into wine, and possibly of the miracles performed in Jerusalem at the feast. His encounter with Jesus was as impactful and life changing as any recorded. Initially, Jesus appeared to turn him off. **Then said Jesus unto him,....** He was given a stern gaze and harsh tone, in a way of reproof for his unbelief, as if he could not heal his son without going down to Capernaum along with him. **"except ye see signs and wonders ye will not believe."** This was the case with the Jews everywhere, both in Judea and Galilee; they required signs and miracles to be performed, in confirmation of Christ's being the Messiah.

The nobleman saith unto him, "Sir,.... In spite of this reproof, and seeming denial, he presses him again, and addressing him in a humble and courteous manner, saying: **come down ere my son die."** Here was a combination of faith and unbelief, he believed that Jesus was able to heal his son, but he still thought that his physical presence was necessary to accomplish it. Nevertheless, he did not need to see it to believe it could happen. The prior testimony of other credible witnesses had already convinced him that Jesus could do for him, what he had done for others.

When Jesus commanded the man to go home, assuring him that his son would not die and his presence was not necessary to accomplish the healing, the man believed the words of Jesus and went about his way. He never questioned or pressed upon Jesus to do anything. He simply took Him at his word and obeyed. What a lesson for the body of Christ today, to take Him at his word and obey. It was unlikely that the man went home immediately, but probably the next morning, being it was late afternoon when the dramatic encounter occurred. As he was returning home to Capernaum, he was met by some of his servants, who had been sent, to inform him that his son had been healed, **and told *him*, saying, "thy son liveth"**. They dispatched as soon as this cure was produced, though they didn't know how or by whom.

> **Then enquired he of them the hour when he began to amend. And they said unto him, Yesterday at the seventh hour the fever left him. (Joh 4:52)**

He was not the least bit surprised, nor was he questioning the truthfulness of the messengers, but simply wanted to compare the timing of the healing. **So the father knew that it was at the same hour,....** exactly, **in that which Jesus said to him, thy son liveth**. He had observed what time of day it was, of his encounter with Jesus; and particularly, when he told him his son was alive and well, and when he took his leave of him; and by comparing the account of his servants, with that, found that things entirely agreed, and that the healing was done exactly at the time, that Jesus spoke the words. He realized that at the moment he believed, was the moment his son was saved.

> **This *is* again the second miracle *that* Jesus did, when he was come out of Judaea into Galilee. (Joh 4:54)**

The healing of the nobleman's son brought to mind an incident when our youngest son Virgil was an infant and was suffering from a very high fever (105°) which brought on convulsions. The child had been feverish all day, was cranky, would neither eat nor hold any fluids. As my wife and I were rushing the child to the emergency room, God spoke into my spirit and told him to pray for the child. Immediately, Mark 16:18 came to his remembrance, **they shall lay hands on the sick, and they shall**

recover. As I pondered the vision in my mind, my wife Daisy spoke and said to me, "turn the truck around, let us go home and pray." "What did you say", I asked? Wanting to be sure that this is what I was hearing from my wife. "The Holy Spirit just spoke to me, and told me to pray for our son", she replied. Immediately, the three were headed back home, although they had been praying to themselves already. By the time they pulled into the driveway of their home, they realized that Virgil was fast asleep, with none of the listlessness and crankiness as before, but sweet sleep. When we went back into the house, we placed the child onto his bed and prayed the prayer of faith over him according to Mark 16:18 and went to bed themselves. I was tempted to check on the infant throughout the night, but refrained. Only looking in on him just to see that he was still asleep. I never touched him to check the fever. Amazingly, when they awake the next morning, there was no fever. Not only was his temperature down to 98.6°, but his diaper rash had disappeared. I responded to my wife, "the Lord was just showing off, look, the diaper rash is gone." It is easy to explain away a broken fever overnight, children's Tylenol is good for that, but Desinex never worked that fast on a diaper rash. It was their first time experiencing divine healing. It was then that the wife said, "the baby actually stopped crying and went to sleep last night at the moment you turned around the truck to go home to pray". As it was with the Nobleman and his son, so it was with this Writer and his wife, at the moment we believed, the victory was won. It was our first significant encounter with Jesus, where we trusted him with the life of our most precious possession, our infant son. As parents, the other five children were loved equally, but there is always something most precious about the baby of the family. This family would believe God as never before, through the raising of six children, establishing careers, planting a church and allowing God to prosper their souls as a testimony to his goodness and power. Ironically, that same infant son, who was the object of divine healing, God used him again in the development of the ministry. My wife and I prayed that the Lord would send us a musician to play at church. One Sunday, the Lord spoke to me and told me to pray over the child's hands that he may play music in His name. So I obeyed the voice of God, prayed once again over my son, this time not for healing, but anointing that he may be used for His glory. Within a few weeks the child was playing as if he had been playing for years. Now, Virgil is a twenty one year old college graduate preparing to enter law school, and still a servant of the Lord.

CHAPTER 5

Sir, I Have No Man (To Help Me)

> After this there was a feast of the Jews; and Jesus went up to Jerusalem. Now there is at Jerusalem by the sheep *market* a pool, which is called in the Hebrew tongue Bethesda, having five porches. In these lay a great multitude of impotent folk, of blind, halt, withered, waiting for the moving of the water. **(Joh 5:1-3)**

Some months later, we find Jesus back in Jerusalem at another feast of the Jews, probably the feast of Passover. Our next significant encounter takes place at the sheep market pool called Bethesda, which in the original Greek meaning "the house of kindness". The narrative describes a motley crew of despicable folk waiting there for the miraculous healing powers rumored to be present in the water. It is not certain if the evangelist is actually stating a historical fact or just repeating the folklore which was reported to him concerning the waters of Bethesda, or wrote it at all. Concerning the moving of the waters, **Earl wrote**, "This last part of verse 3 and all of verse 4 are not found in the two third century papyrus manuscripts of John's Gospel (66 and 75)- made only about 100 years after John was written- in our only two fourth century manuscripts or two of the four manuscripts from the fifth century. It is completely clear to any honest observer that this legend, about an angel who came down and "troubled the water," was not part of the original Gospel of John. It was added centuries later to explain the man's reference in verse 7." But, what is not subject to speculation is this, there was a crowd there and Jesus came. The regular use of the sheep pool was to wash the entrails of the sacrifices, so the pool was a bloody, smelly mess. For people to wait around in such an atmosphere under such conditions, spoke of their desperation. The afflictions of those at the pool are representative of the conditions of many "church folk" who assemble at their churches (houses of kindness) waiting for some angel or Pastor to make the waters move for them and bring some kind of relief to their empty and defeated lives.

The Impotent

The Evangelist describes a multitude of folk, all with special needs and conditions. The **impotent,** which Strong's defines as astheneo (*as-then-eh'-o*); to *be feeble* (in any sense): be diseased, impotent folk (man), (be) sick, (be, be made) weak. They **lacked power** and were **impotent,** no power to do the work of ministry. Jesus said in John 15:5 "without me you can do nothing". They were impotent because they were following a man and not God. The text says they were waiting for an angel to stir the water. The word translated angel also means messenger. It is the same word used in the Book of Revelation in the letters to the seven churches of Asia Minor in chapters 2 and 3. In other words, the people were waiting for the pastors to do something that could only be achieved by the Holy Spirit. The water is representative of the word. The Bible says we are cleaned by the washing of regeneration by the word. Unheeded Word, just sitting there on the tables of their hearts left them powerless to glorify God. They are powerless because they are looking for a man to move them and not the Spirit.

These feeble folk not only lacked the ability to do the work of ministry, they also lacked the ability to do for themselves. People who lack the ability to perform activities of daily living without the assistance of others are generally classified as the disabled. Activities of daily living such as cooking, cleaning, bathing, toileting, etc. are activities most people take for granted. For those who lack the potency to perform these tasks, life can be a challenge. Impotence is also a term also used to describe a man's inability to participate in the act of procreation; those who lack the ability to reproduce after their own kind. This could also apply to other types of power, in addition to men with no physical power, also no economic power; the disenfranchised who lacked political power; the uneducated who lacked mental or intellectual power and the cowards who lack moral power.

➢ Economic Impotence

A lack of economic power creates all sorts of problems. The rich ruleth over the poor and the borrower is servant to the lender. People with less stable incomes generally have lower credit scores, which means they will pay higher rates of interest for the same goods and services than those with good credit scores and more stable incomes. Nehemiah describes the situation in his day thusly,

> *Some* also there were that said, We have mortgaged our lands, vineyards, and houses, that we might buy corn, because of the dearth. There were also that said, We have borrowed money for the king's tribute, *and that upon* our lands and vineyards. Yet now our flesh *is* as the flesh of our brethren, our children as their children: and, lo, we bring into bondage our sons and our daughters to be servants, and *some* of our daughters are brought unto bondage *already:* neither *is it* in our power *to redeem them;* for other men have our lands and vineyards. And I was very angry when I heard their cry and these words. (Neh 5:3-6)

In the situation in Nehemiah, the rich Jews were taking advantage of the poor Jews and subjecting their own people to economic hardship. In the text, the people had mortgaged their lands, (long term debt) to buy consumer goods (short term, expendable assets) and to pay their taxes. One of the first rules of financial planning is avoid using long term debt to pay for short term expenses. They had also sold their sons into slavery and pimped out their daughters to pay their debts, with no possibility of redemption. This was an extreme case but it describes the life of economic impotence.

When the financial system failed in 2008, it created world-wide chaos and panic. A boom in the financial system was created by an overheated housing market where the government encouraged and incentivized financial institutions to make home loans to risky borrowers. Many of the loans were adjustable rate loans that escalated in rate and payment amount after three to five years. Most of the borrowers simply refinanced at the adjustment date, the banks made more money on the refis, the homeowner stayed at the same payment, but the principle balance increased or remained the same. The home values increased because of increased demand for housing and many homeowners actually cashed out the increased equity in their homes and spent the money on consumer goods and luxury items. The financial institutions created investment instruments based on the loan portfolios and sold them as investment grade products to other institutions and institutional investors. Because these instruments paid such a high rate of return and appeared safe being backed by the value of the homes, which secured the mortgages, they appealed to a great many of investors. The problem occurred when the bubble burst. A large proportion of mortgages came due at the same time and many of the homeowners were unable to refinance as before. They had spent the loan proceeds on frivolous expenditures and had no savings or financial cushion. As long as the foreclosure rate on property remained at less the 2%, the loan portfolios would be safe, but when the foreclosure rate exceeded that threshold, the market was challenged. When the foreclosure rate exceeded 10%, the market collapsed and the foreclosures cascaded as a tsunami across the economic landscape, wiping out fortunes in its wake. Companies, institutions, and individuals heavily invested in the mortgage backed securities found the securities were not worth the paper they were printed on.

The problem was this, the securities were sold as investment grade (AAA+) based on the credit ratings of the institutions which issued them, rather than the bad credit scores of the actual homeowners (DDD-) upon whom repayment of the loans would come. Companies such as Lehman Brothers, Bear Stearns, AIG, Wachovia, and many of the largest and seemingly most powerful financial institutions in the world had large amounts of these securities in their investment portfolios. The banks holding these securities on their books as short term assets appeared able to meet the regulatory requirements for loan loss reserves. When the value of these securities collapsed, so did the loan reserves and the banks went out of business because the federal government had to assume the liability for the deposits that make up the amount of money available to lend. With no more money to lend more foreclosures occurred because fewer banks had money to lend to cash strapped homeowners. On top of that, the value of the homes plummeted creating a situation where the homeowners actually owed more on the homes than they were worth, which exasperated the problem; which led to more foreclosures. Business shut downs, layoffs, downsizing and economic recession ensued. The people who were fortunate enough and wise enough to avoid investing in the questionable instruments found themselves in position to buy properties for cents on the dollar. The stock market lost half of its value in less than six months and many people lost not only their homes, but also their pensions, retirements and their economic freedom. The need for economic power was never more apparent than during this period of financial turbulence. Nonetheless, it paled in comparison to the economic impotence of the remnant Jews during the days of Nehemiah. The economically impotent in this day are powerless to sustain the work of the church and have caused many churches to resort to fundraising gimmicks in order to remain viable. Because of massive consumer debt, many church members are unable to tithe, support missions, sponsor charitable activities or many of the activities that are vital to the work of ministry, including paying the light bill at the House of God, or even pay the Pastor's salary.

➤ Political Impotence

Political impotence is characterized by disenfranchisement, tyranny and futility. The politically impotent cannot practice self determination. He lacks the opportunity to effect any changes to the circumstances of his existence. It is ironic that America was founded out of a response to tyranny. The writers of the Unanimous Declaration of Independence of the United States of America wrote their appeal to the Supreme Judge of the world (God) for the rectitude of its intentions. In addition to a gospel preacher, I am also a high school teacher who gave the assignment of writing a research paper comparing the holocaust of the Jews under Nazi tyranny and the plight of the American Blacks during the Jim Crowe era. Much was gleaned from this exercise.

The Jews Under Nazi Tyranny:

Regarding the Jews, they were systematically stripped of political power by the Nazis. Following the big war (WWI), Germany had taken a beating geo-politically for siding with the losing side (Ottomans, Austria-Hungary, Balkans, Italy) and leaving its economy in ruins. Exacerbated by the great depression, Germany needed a fall guy and they chose the Jews. The Nazis came into power blaming the Jews for all the problems facing Germany. Historically, because the Jews maintained wealth and economic power, they managed to maintain political power, even during the war and the depression. However, once the Nazis came to power in Germany, they enacted laws making it easier to take the property and rights of the Jews. By 1936, the political emasculation of the Jews was complete in Germany under Hitler and the Nazis.

Reconstruction:

Conversely, After reconstruction (1865-1877), the political landscape in America had dramatically changed. The freed slaves managed to make economic and political progress during the reconstruction period. The plantation system in the old south had been ruined and the Carpetbaggers came in to economically exploit the defeated south. In ten states coalitions of freedmen, recent black and white arrivals from the North (carpetbaggers), and white Southerners who supported Reconstruction (scalawags) cooperated to form Republican biracial state governments. They introduced various reconstruction programs, including the founding of public schools in most states for the first time, and the establishment of charitable institutions. They raised taxes, which historically had been low as planters preferred to make private investments for their own purposes; offered massive aid to support railroads to improve transportation and shipping. Conservative opponents charged that Republican regimes were marred by widespread corruption. Violent opposition towards freedmen and whites who supported Reconstruction emerged in numerous localities under the name of the Ku Klux Klan, a secret vigilante organization, which led to federal intervention by President Ulysses S. Grant in 1871 that closed down the Klan. Conservative white Democrats calling themselves "Redeemers" regained control state by state, sometimes using fraud and violence to control state elections.

The end of Reconstruction was a staggered process, and the period of Republican control ended at different times in different states. With the Compromise of 1877, Army intervention in the South ceased and Republican control collapsed in the last three state governments in the South. This was followed by a period that white Southerners labeled Redemption, in which white-dominated state legislatures enacted Jim Crow laws and (after 1890) disfranchised most blacks and many poor whites through a combination of constitutional amendments and electoral laws. The white democrat Southerners' memory of Reconstruction played a major role in imposing the system of <u>white supremacy</u> and <u>second-class citizenship</u> for blacks, known as the age of <u>Jim Crow</u>. The Democratic Party monopolized the "<u>New South</u>" into the 1960s, when the civil rights and voting rights of African Americans were finally protected and enforced under new civil rights legislation. (Infopedia)

America's Blacks Under Jim Crow:

After reconstruction ended, all the political gains made by blacks were systematically eradicated by malicious white southerners envious of those gains made while they suffered as a spoil of war. Through intimidation and unjust legislation, within a few short years voting rights, representation and political participation were all gone. The use of literacy tests, pole taxes, gerrymandering and many other devices including lynching, were being utilized with the purpose of disenfranchising black voters and denying any participation in the political process. In the eighty second Psalm, the divine person asked the question, "How long will ye judge unjustly and accept the persons of the wicked?" This, calling into account the systemic injustice suffered by the people of God at the hand of those in power. He makes his plea to the judges of the earth to, "**Defend the poor and fatherless: do justice to the afflicted and needy. Deliver the poor and needy: rid *them* out of the hand of the wicked**." It is clear that God does not hold blameless the minions of tyranny, whether it be the Nazis inflicting it upon the Jews, or the southern whites upon the blacks. Free will is hardwired into the soul of every man. During these dark periods of human history, political impotence was imposed upon God's people, and they too waited for the stirring of the water.

➤ Academic Impotence

The academically impotent are the uneducated. It is easy to see the harm of being uneducated. Prior to emancipation, in most southern states, it was against the law to educate a negro. The slave masters understood the best way to keep the slaves under control was to keep them physically strong but dependent upon them. After slavery ended, motivation for maintaining the status quo regarding education remained, "if you keep them illiterate and ignorant you can still control them". It is astonishing that in many communities, the graduation rate of African American students is less than 50%; meaning, those affected will be consigned to a life of academic impotence, which will lead to economic impotence. Although all of society's ills can be attributed to one cause, sin, even still these ills can be mitigated by getting a good education. The educated man will earn more money in his life time than the uneducated. Even the educated sinner will earn more than the uneducated.

Below are statistics taken from the 2011 Statistical Abstract of the United States Bureau of Census. (median incomes)

Measure	Some High School	High school graduate	Some college	Associate's degree	Bachelor's degree or higher	Bachelor's degree	Master's degree	Professional degree	Doctorate degree
Persons, age 25+ w/ earnings	$20,321	$26,505	$31,056	$35,009	$49,303	$43,143	$52,390	$82,473	$69,432
Male, age 25+ w/ earnings	$24,192	$32,085	$39,150	$42,382	$60,493	$52,265	$67,123	$100,000	$78,324
Female, age 25+ w/ earnings	$15,073	$21,117	$25,185	$29,510	$40,483	$36,532	$45,730	$66,055	$54,666
Persons, age 25+, employed full-time	$25,039	$31,539	$37,135	$40,588	$56,078	$50,944	$61,273	$100,000	$79,401

Income distribution

Race,	WHITE	BLACK	ASIAN	HISPANIC
	$65000	$39936	$73368	$40466
Dropout rates	4.8%	9.9%	4.4 %	18.3%
Bachelor's degrees	30.1%	16.2%	51.3%	15.9%

➤ A Mind is a Terrible Thing to Waste

In viewing the aforementioned statistics, it is apparent that the earning power of an educated person far exceeds that of the uneducated. This statistic holds true across every ethnic or gender line. Although it is not the purpose of this book to explain every variation in the correlation between earnings and education, it does attempt to show the futility one should expect in life once he or she forgoes, for whatever reason, an education. On the average, the high school graduate should expect to earn 20% more than the drop-out. The college graduate should expect to earn $20000 more annually than the high school graduate, while those who earn their masters degree will earn another 25%. One alarming trend noted in the data is the disparity between the races, regardless of education. According to the Census Bureau, the median income of white families was almost 40% higher than that of black and Hispanic families. Considering the educational attainment reported, such a trend could be expected because while 30% of whites reported earning a Bachelor's degree, only 16.2% of blacks and 15.9% of Hispanics earned such degrees. Also, the dropout rate of blacks was reported at 9.9%, 18.3% for Hispanics, 4.8% for whites and 4.4% for Asians. The drop-out rate represents those who did not complete the requirements for attaining a high school diploma by age 24. The pool of Bethesda, which was supposed to be the house of kindness, became a gathering place for the desperate. If it was located in America, surely the educationally impotent gathering there would have included a higher percentage of blacks and Hispanics.

> **Moral Impotence**

Moral impotence can be characterized by the inability to **do justly.** In Micah 6:8, the Prophet asks the question, "........**and what does the Lord require of thee,**" which he answers in the question, "**but to do justly, and to love mercy, and to walk humbly with thy God?**" The morally impotent person is fighting a losing battle in his mind against his flesh. His earthy desires will always overwhelm whatever in him might point out the error of his ways. In his book, <u>Mere Christianity</u>, C.S.Lewis, while comparing individual humans and their relationship to each other as a fleet of ships at sea and as members of an orchestra, wrote this concerning morality. "Morality, then, seems to be concerned with three things. Firstly, with fair play and harmony between individuals; Secondly, with what might be called tidying up or harmonizing the things inside each individual. Thirdly, with the general purpose of human life as a whole: what man was made for; what course the whole fleet out to be on; what tune the conductor of the band wants to play. ....Almost all people at all times have agreed (in theory) that human beings ought to be honest and kind and helpful to one another. But though it is natural to begin with all that, if our thinking about morality stops there, we might just as well not have thought at all. Unless we go to the second thing—the tidying up inside each human being—we are only deceiving ourselves." **Lewis** understood the natural human tendency to remain on the surface and not deal with the core issue of innate sin inherent in all men. In mustering up a level of morality that pleases God, like the woman at Jacob's well, we too have nothing to draw with and will find ourselves waiting for a man to miraculously move the stagnant and sullied water.

The Blind

Also at the sheep pool, were the **blind** Those who **lacked discernment** and were spiritually **blind** might also be included in this group waiting for a miracle. Without physical vision, a person would be in need of someone to guide them. They would always be susceptible to injury due to slips, falls, trips or other possible hazards including duplicitous guides. In spite of these hazards, it is even more hazardous to be spiritually blind, with an inability to see the hand of God. Without the ability to see God moving in your own life can create a lot of missed opportunities. **Where there is no vision, the people perish. (Prov 29:18a)** Without a revelation from God, the hopes, dreams, aspirations and ambitions of men will die. Harriet Tubman was quoted, *"I freed thousands of slaves. I could have freed thousands more if they had known they were slaves."* Apparently, the slaves were accustomed to the status quo, and those born into slavery, knew of nothing else. The white masters using the techniques taught by William Lynch perpetuated the hold on the blacks by manipulating them into turning on each other and depending on their white masters for sustenance. The blacks were blinded to the reality that they would be better off if they looked out for and trusted one another, rather than every man for himself and trusting ole "Massa". When anyone is trusting in someone who does not have their best interest at heart, they are destined for trouble.

Possibly the worst case of a people being victimized by duplicitous leadership occurred in 1978 at Jonestown Guyana. Over three decades ago an unusual series of events led to the deaths of more than 900 people in the middle of a South American jungle. Though dubbed a "massacre," what transpired at Jonestown on November 18, 1978, was to some extent done willingly, making the mass suicide all the more disturbing. The Jonestown cult (officially named the "People's Temple") was founded in 1955 by Indianapolis preacher James Warren Jones. Jones, who had no formal theological training, based his liberal ministry on a combination of religious and socialist philosophies.

After relocating to California in 1965, the church continued to grow in membership and began advocating their left-wing political ideals more actively. With an I.R.S. investigation and a great deal of negative press mounting against the radical church, Jones urged his congregation to join him in a new, isolated community where they could escape American capitalism—and criticism—and practice a more communal way of life. In 1977, Jones and many of his followers relocated to Jonestown, located on a tract of land the People's Temple had purchased and begun to develop in Guyana three years earlier. Relatives of cult members soon grew concerned and requested that the U.S. government rescue what they believed to be brainwashed victims living in concentration camp-like conditions under Jones's power.

In November 1978, California Congressman Leo Ryan arrived in Guyana to survey Jonestown and interview its inhabitants. After reportedly having his life threatened by a Temple member during the first day of his visit, Ryan decided to cut his trip short and return to the U.S. with some Jonestown residents who wished to leave. As they boarded their plane, a group of Jones's guards opened fire on them, killing Ryan and four others.

Some members of Ryan's party escaped, however. Upon learning this, Jones told his followers that Ryan's murder would make it impossible for their commune to continue functioning. Rather than return to the United States, the People's Temple would preserve their church by making the ultimate sacrifice: their own lives. Jones's 912 followers were given a deadly concoction of a purple drink mixed with cyanide, sedatives, and tranquilizers. Jones apparently shot himself in the head. Because all of those people were mislead by a Charlatan, under the guise of spiritual leader, they sacrificed their lives. They blindly followed Jones to Guyana expecting him to stir the waters only to lose everything they owned, including their lives.

The Halt

Next to the blind were the **halt**, that is, *limping:* - cripple, halt, lame. They **lacked doctrinal discipline** and were **halt** or crippled emotionally as well as physically. These were also the people who lacked movement or mobility. Many have the skills to do better, but they are stuck in a rut and can't seem to get out. They are stuck on a dead end job with no opportunity to advance. Some were crippled by disease, some by poor choices, and others by harsh and difficult circumstances. Whether it is the glass ceiling, the closed door or the brick wall, the person is stuck in their current situation with no apparent relief in sight. Whatever one's condition in life might have been, as long as the status quo remains, no improvement would or could be made. A lack of mobility can damage the spirit of a man as much as a lack of power or a lack of vision.

According the Bureau of Census, with the exception of Hispanics, every ethnic minority group, which immigrated to America, attained a higher degree of education than the American born of that group. This is significant because it speaks to opportunity. While those people groups were stuck in their native lands, the opportunities were limited and hopelessness abounded. Once those minorities arrived in America, they appreciated the opportunities available for them. They would work harder to achieve educational and professional goals that were only a dream in their native lands, while their American born counterparts may have taken things for granted. In the narrative, one such person waiting at the pool, had been there twelve years waiting for something to happen. Imagine the despair of a soul on a job, for twelve years waiting for a raise that never materialized, but he was stuck there because he may have a criminal record that prevents him from finding a better job. Tom Phelan, Branch Sales Manager for Bankers Life and Casualty Company Casselberry Office, regarding new recruits said, "I always look for people who have a PHD, not people who are Doctors of Philosophy, but people who are **poor, hungry and driven.**" Phelan looks for people who were previously in dead end jobs with limited earnings potential and low advancement opportunities and present to them an opportunity to earn more and advance as high as they want to go. His target recruit would probably not be hanging around a proverbial pool of Bethesda.

The lack of doctrinal discipline also hinders a person from making progress because they are tossed to and fro with every wind of doctrine.

Church hoppers are prone to experiencing stagnated spiritual growth. The hoppers never allow the biblical principals emphasized and taught by the present spiritual leader to take hold. Before all the underlying principals are laid out and subsequent teachings are added, these people have run off and taken up at another church, ministry or system of philosophical thought. This could be compared to someone going through a twelve step recovery program and quitting by the fifth step; then hooking up with another Pastor who is going through the forty days of purpose program and quitting that program after the twenty-forth day. While both those and many other programs are commendable and have allowed people to experience progress and victory in many areas of life, none will be successful if a person quits too soon and starts another before he finishes the first.

Those at the pool, unlike the church hoppers previously referred to, physically remained in one place, the bigger tragedy is people remaining in one place or at the same level spiritually because they never obeyed the doctrine they were taught. Possibly, there every week, attending every meeting, experiencing every worship moment and observing every manifestation of the power of God, but never heeding the truth being fed to them. There will never be spiritual growth apart from obedience to the Word of God. Like Hophni and Phineas, the sons of the Priest Eli in the Old Testament book of I Samuel. They undoubtedly heard their father preach the Word of God daily and observe him administer the sacrifices faithfully, yet because of unbelief and hardness of heart, they were unmoved. The scripture identified them as Son's of Belial (the devil).

The Withered

Next to the halt were the withered. **Men** with withered hands and limbs. The hand represents not only resources, but also, the ability to accomplish, create and build wealth. They **lacked influence** on the culture around them and the resources to impact that culture; they were **withered**. In order to make an impact on the world in with you live, you must have some resources to invest into your own life and the lives of other people. The writer of Ecclesiastes understood this principal when he wrote in the eleventh chapter; **Cast thy bread upon the waters: for thou shalt find it after many days. Give a portion to seven, and also to eight; for thou knowest not what evil shall be upon the earth.**

You must have some seed to sow in order to expect any kind of harvest. The hand metaphorically is as the primary resource for building wealth and escaping poverty, but it dried up. Usually, plants wither because of a lack of water or nourishment. It is the first sign that it is about to die. The psalmist put it this way; **And he shall be like a tree planted by the rivers of waters, that bringeth forth his fruit in his season. His leaf also shall not wither, and whatsoever he doeth will prosper. The ungodly are not so, but are like the chaff which the wind drives away. (Psalm 1:1-3)** The withered is someone who at some point had a source of power, but no longer. The withered is someone who once possessed the resources to have, maintain and export the abundant life but no more. For whatever the reason, the resources dried up.

One of the biggest drains on the resources of the believer (the heathen also for that matter) is debt. During the boom years of the 80's and 90's, credit was relatively easy to obtain. The economy was expanding, employment was relatively high and the incentive to get people to spend money motivated the credit issuers to seek out new customers. The average American held two or more credit cards. It was not uncommon for a cardholder to pay the minimum amount due on one card with the cash advance from another card. The card issuers would often offer the opportunity to transfer the balance of currently held cards onto a brand new card with a low teaser rate. The cardholder would make the transfer, but rather than cut up the old paid off card they would eventually max out the new card, then max out the old previously paid off cards and be on the hook for even more debt. Once the teaser rates have expired, they would be stuck with punitive rates which would often lead to bankruptcy. There are many other reasons for the drying up of resources but they will be dealt with in another book. Nonetheless, many **lacked initiative** and were sitting around waiting for a man to do for them what they could do for themselves. But there was one there who caught the eye of the Master.

Jesus spotted him out of the multitude. There was nothing physically wrong with the rest of them. Their problem was spiritual. But this particular man's condition truly was real and he simply made the mistake of depending on folk who looked like him. Many church folk look the part of true believers and the novice could not tell the difference. He thought he needed someone to trouble the water, but what he really needed was a dramatic encounter with Jesus.

John 5:6 When Jesus saw him lie,.... In such a helpless condition: **and knew that he had been now a long time,** *in that case*, or "in his disease", even seven years before Christ was born; which is a proof of his omniscience: the words may be literally rendered, "that he had had much time"; or as the Arabic version, "that he had had many years"; that is had lived many years, and was now an old man; he had his disorder eight and thirty years, and which seems from <u>Joh 5:14</u> to have arisen from some sin of his, perhaps from a vicious course of living, perhaps intemperance; so that he might be a middle aged man, when this distemper first seized him, and therefore must be now stricken in years.

He saith unto him, "wilt thou be made whole?" The question is asked, not as if it was a doubt, whether he was desirous of it, or not; why else would he be there? Perhaps he wanted to raise in the man an expectation of a cure, and to draw the attention of the people to it. Perhaps his sense and meaning was, wilt thou be made whole on this day, which was the Sabbath, or hast thou faith that thou shall be made whole in this way, or by me? **Sir, I have no man,....**Instead of *saying* he wished to be cured, he just simply talks of his own futility, and how helpless and hopeless he was. Yet not quite because here he is at the pool, waiting on something which seemed of no use, but Jesus was there.

More Controversy

> And immediately the man was made whole, and took up his bed, and walked: and on the same day was the sabbath. The Jews therefore said unto him that was cured, It is the sabbath day: it is not lawful for thee to carry *thy* bed.   (Joh 5:9-10)

Rise, take up thy bed, and walk. "Immediately" he did so. "He *spake* and it was *done*." The slinging of his portable couch over his shoulders was designed to show the perfection of the cure. The thing that once held him, was now being carried by him. Typical of the reactions to the ministry of Jesus, more controversy arose. When the Evangelist identified the antagonists of Jesus, he referred to them as "the Jews." This reference primarily described the Scribes, Pharisees, Sadducees, Sanhedrin or other temple officials. Since practically everyone in Jerusalem was by race, a Jew, with the exception a few Roman or other Gentile inhabitants of the area, this distinction should be made. These were the same Jews Nicodemus hoped to avoid in his dramatic encounter in the dead of night. The healed man walking through the streets of Jerusalem carrying his bed on the Sabbath caused a serious uproar. **It is the Sabbath day: it is not lawful for thee to carry *thy* bed.** It would have been more preferable for the Jews if the man had remained in his cripple state and the Sabbath to be kept than for God to be glorified by his healing. **He answered them,....** That is, the formerly impotent man, who was now made whole, replied to the Jews, "**he that made me whole, the same said unto me, take up thy bed and walk.**" His implication was, if this man had the ability to do what only God could do, then it seemed appropriate to dispense with the Sabbath and comply with whatever order he commanded. **Then asked they him,....** Suspecting who had made him whole, and gave him this order: "**what man is that which said unto thee, take up thy bed and walk?**" Completely ignoring the cure, their focus was on the fact that this cure was wrought on the Sabbath. Rather than give glory to Christ, their only interest was to spread rancor and ignominy to His name. **And he that was healed, wist not who he was,....** He had never seen, and perhaps had never heard of Christ before, and so he did not know him and besides, Christ departed the area so quickly, it gave him no opportunity to talk to him, or so much as to ask him who he was. **for Jesus had conveyed himself away.**

Afterward Jesus findeth him in the temple, probably on the same day. It would be safe to assume that a man who had been infirmed for thirty eight years would relish the opportunity to return thanks to God for his healing. In his desperation, the man was willing to wait outside the temple for relief that never came. He had been willing to expose himself to the stench and filth of the pool of Bethesda, now felt right at home inside the temple. He had felt at home keeping company with the other desperate losers who also had no power, no mobility, no vision, no resources, or no hope. All expecting some movement to change their situation, but he had a dramatic encounter with Jesus who saw beneath the exterior and spoke directly into his spirit. But he was not through with him;......, **and said unto him, behold thou art made whole**; like the leper after having been cleansed returned to say thanks, this man must have pleased Jesus in seeing him at the temple. Unlike others, who showed no honor in response to his miracles, this man's response would have been appropriate for all men regardless of the times in which they lived. What was interesting here, Jesus never asked for, nor called him by name. He didn't need to call his name because his identity was about to change. He had become a new creation in Christ, old things, his impotency, his hopelessness, his desperation had been passed away and **behold**, all things, including his vigor, his strength, his outlook on life would be made new. Having experienced the manifold blessings of God, he was thankful, as all men should be. An attitude of gratitude always pleases the heart of God.

Something Has to Change

Behold..........getting the man's attention as to what was about to transpire. Jesus had begun a good work and now was poised to see it come to completion. His next statement although directed to the man, needs to be heeded by all men. This is the requirement of every man who has been delivered from bondage by God's mighty hand. **Sin no more**; suggesting that as all diseases of the body spring from sin, so had his. Being physically healed was not enough, Jesus knew that in order for this man or any man to experience all that God has for him, the inner man must be healed; healed from the disease of sin. The past life that brought about his impotency had to be replaced. **Lest a worse thing come unto thee**; God could allow a worse disease, or a greater affliction, than he had yet done; either in this world, or the world to come.

Although this man's sin is not identified, his situation was not unlike that of the modern day addict. The addict becomes co-dependent upon others to not only meet their own needs, but also to value their own worth. In his book, *12 Steps With Jesus,* which deals with dependency, Don Williams wrote, "Disbelieving his own adequacy, recoiling from challenge, the addict welcomes control from outside himself as the ideal state of affairs. Out of insecurity, these addicts fail to act, they only react." Williams' explanation is exemplified in the behavior of the man at the pool who was asked of Jesus, "do you want to be made whole?", his response was not an immediate yes, which obviously was the case, but a lame, "I have no man to help ..." In his sinfulness, possibly addictive state, this man would never look within himself for resolve, but always on the outside. Unfortunately, those outside were as messed up as him and they too needed a savior. This encounter only exposed the Jews as the self righteous hypocrites they really were and the hopelessness of going through life without an awareness of the grace and power of God. But it also revealed to the desperate, including he who had been healed, as well as the readers of this book, of the opportunities inherent in a relationship with the savior.

CHAPTER 6

There is a Lad There

> After these things Jesus went over the sea of Galilee, which is *the sea of* Tiberias. And a great multitude followed him, because they saw his miracles which he did on them that were diseased.
> (Joh 6:1-2)

A year had passed since the dramatic encounters surrounding the Jerusalem feast of the previous chapter and the notoriety of Jesus had increased dramatically. His fame had spread to the point where his customary practice of retreating to a deserted place to pray and refresh himself was becoming increasingly more difficult. Because of his fame, **a great multitude followed him,....** From several cities and towns in Galilee, where he had been preaching and working miracles, **because they saw his miracles which he did on them that were diseased.** Apparently, the crowds did not come so much because of his message or his doctrine, but as curiosity seekers. Some even came seeking to be healed. But their motives, though selfish at this point did not deter Jesus. Nor did it cause him to lose his resolve to carry out his mission. Another attempt to get away was interrupted. Jesus had gone up into the mountain to continue the training of the twelve, but a crowd followed him there. Apparently, Jesus was in a moment of prayer, and behold, as he lifted his eyes he saw this great company of desperate people. **He saith unto Philip.......** he directed his discourse to him particularly, because he was an inhabitant of Bethsaida, near their current location, and therefore might be best able to answer the following question. **Whence shall we buy bread, that these may eat?** It was still the objective of Jesus to utilize

51

the time for the continuation of the training of the twelve, nevertheless, this uninvited crowd had presented him with the opportunity to teach a principle that would greatly enhance the effectiveness of all of his disciples and servants (in that day as well as this).

Conventional wisdom would suggest that Philip would have the answer to that question, but the answer would not be the product of conventional wisdom, but as a result of an application of biblical principles. Philip's response exposed the insufficiency of human effort and the carnality of his own mind. **"Two hundred pennyworth of bread is not sufficient for them, that every one of them may take a little."** Not only did Philip's response expose his own, inadequacies, it also provided the Christ with an opportunity to continue his role as professor, along with the opportunity for another servant to display a quality that the church is woefully lacking, which is, the quality of availability. **One of his disciples, Andrew, Simon Peter's brother,....** Who along with his brother Peter, as well as Philip, were of Bethsaida, having heard what Christ said to Philip, and what His reply, **saith unto him;** to Christ, with but little more faith than Philip, assuming of course that Philip might possess some, if any. **There is a lad here,....** The identity of the lad was not certain, nor was it important. What was important, was the fact that Andrew spotted him among the five thousand souls they had encountered. The significance of the encounter was not the fact that five thousand people might show up uninvited or unexpected, but that there was an apparent need along with an apparent impossibility, yet the solution to this dilemma was right in their midst. Just as significant was the fact that it was Andrew who saw the possibility.

First of all, the dilemma posed was a preponderance of people with no possible way to care for their needs. The principle is this, people will have a difficult time receiving the Word if their temporal needs remain unfilled. Before Jesus preached to them, he wanted to put them in a position, where they could actually receive what he had to say. A lesson for the church today, If people are worried about the affairs of this world, in the absence of much biblical faith, they will have a difficult time hearing from God. Typical of Andrew, with his spiritual antennae in array, was aware of a hidden resource that Philip never saw. There was a little boy with his lunch and Jesus was there. The second significance of this encounter was this; Even though Andrew was not a central figure on the scene, he still was paying attention and remained aware of what was going on. Unlike his friend Philip who managed to get the direct attention of the Master, yet had no answer when it was required of him, Andrew on the other hand was available to act at the moment needed most. Andrew's ego allowed him to function at the highest level in spite of not having a major role in the program. The lad was also significant in that not only did he make himself available for the Master's use, but he relinquished his small resource, his lunch, consisting of five barley loaves and two small fish, for the greater good. What were essentially five biscuits and two sardines in the hand of Jesus was more than enough. Andrew never imagined it to be sufficient, yet it was all there was. Of course, Andrew never imagined the waterpots would be sufficient either, but he witnessed them come forth with wine. As long as Jesus was in the midst, there would be no crisis which can't be managed.

> And Jesus took the loaves; and when he had given thanks, he distributed to the disciples, and the disciples to them that were set down; and likewise of the fishes as much as they would. When they were filled, he said unto his disciples, Gather up the fragments that remain, that nothing be lost. Therefore they gathered *them* together, and filled twelve baskets with the fragments of the five barley loaves, which remained over and above unto them that had eaten. (Joh 6:11-13)

After this tremendous encounter which not only demonstrated the power of Christ and the possibilities inherent in Him, but it also provoked the people into thinking about the possibilities of a life without Roman rule. All of these dramatic encounters with Jesus produced emotional reactions that ranged from amazement, to wonder, as you will later see, to rage. One emotional reaction which was also produced was emboldening. The typical behavior of the Jews regarding Roman occupation was placid docility. In other words, they knew how to avoid a beat-down. They quickly learned of the Roman heavy handedness to those conquered peoples who dared to defy the rule of Caesar and offered no open defiance. Secretly, they hated the Romans, but wouldn't dare challenge them and up until then, not even think about it.

Then those men, when they had seen the miracle that Jesus did, said, This is of a truth that prophet that should come into the world. When Jesus therefore perceived that they would come and take him by force, to make him a king, he departed again into a mountain himself alone. (Joh 6:14-15)

Having perceived that Jesus was that true prophet that should come, Messiah, emboldened the masses to the point that they were willing to openly defy Rome and proclaim Jesus to be their king. Doing so would bring down the wrath of the Romans but they were willing to risk it because Messiah was there. Without this newfound bravery, the people would have been content to accept the status quo and accept Roman domination indefinitely. The five-thousand's dramatic encounter with Jesus which brought about emboldening, led to a shift in doctrinal emphasis on the part of Jesus. Since there were so many unbelievers in the crowd, in order to accomplish the divine purpose of the Father, the Son of Man needed to weed out those whose only reason for being there was to be entertained, amused or even amazed. There were those who wanted to make him their king for the purpose of driving out the Romans, not to become lord over their souls. It was them who needed winnowing out. Those onlookers whose purpose was self interest needed an epiphany of sorts to bring about a self evaluation. Until a man fully examines his own heart, he will always be in delusion. F.B.Meyer wrote, "There is no greater enemy of the highest usefulness than the presence of the flesh in our activities.......We have to encounter it in our unregenerate life, when its passions reveal themselves, brooking no restraint." Meyer would surely understand the Lord's rationale for dealing with the crowds in the manner he chose. By ratcheting up the theology and broadening the scope of his doctrine and by placing a much stronger emphasis on submission to and assimilation of the principles of His Word, He was forcing the listeners to come to terms with the shallowness of their commitment and their self seeking purposes for following him.

In an effort to accomplish his task amidst the throng, Jesus executed the most amazing misdirect ever recorded. He sent his disciples ahead by boat. As they disappeared into the darkness of the sea, he apparently went into the opposite direction alone and afoot. Somehow he managed to elude the crowd still hell-bent on making him king. After the disciples had rowed over three miles out into a very rough sea, their encounter was the most dramatic of all. Jesus appeared unto them walking on the sea. To say they were overcome by fear would be an extreme understatement, but once they recognized that it is Jesus, His very presence allayed their fears, so much so that even Peter walked on the water for a moment, a fact not mentioned here by John.

> So when they had rowed about five and twenty or thirty furlongs, they see Jesus walking on the sea, and drawing nigh unto the ship: and they were afraid. But he saith unto them, It is I; be not afraid. (Joh 6:19-20)

As was customary for Jesus whenever he returned to Capernaum from a campaign, he went into the Synagogue and taught. It was there in the Synagogue where the next dramatic encounter occurred. The crowd from the previous evening anticipating that Jesus would emerge from his mountain getaway and rejoin his disciples whom he had already sent ahead, were awaiting His return. They were still of the mindset of making him king. When Jesus never emerged, they made a very diligent search to look for Him. Knowing that there was only one boat available and seeing the disciples depart without Him, they could not fathom where He might be or how he managed to leave without transport. Nevertheless, anticipating that he would rejoin the disciples who had departed to Capernaum, they made their way there also. In the words of Matthew Henry, "those that would find Jesus must go forth by the footsteps of the flock." Whatever weakness the visible church may possess, It is still the most likely place to find Jesus.

Somehow, along the way, the crowd must have gone through some sort of catharsis, because the notion of making him king was no longer on the agenda. Upon arrival at the Synagogue, and seeing him there teaching, their immediate response was, **"Rabbi"**.

> And when they had found him on the other side of the sea, they said unto him, Rabbi, when camest thou hither? (Joh 6:25)

Gone, was notion of making him king. By referring to Him as Rabbi, their teacher, they must have recognized his unwillingness to cooperate with their agenda, because they made no mention of it. "**When camest thou hither?**" "When did you get here?", was their question, but what they were probably thinking was, "how did you get here?" What was peculiar here was the fact that the true disciples, having braved a tempestuous sea, upon His word preceded to go where He commanded. Upon doing so were given the privilege of witnessing Him miraculously walk on water, while the other group whose purpose was less than noble, having been the beneficiary of the miracle of the loaves and fishes could not fathom the mode by which He came to be into Capernaum, just as they could not or did not comprehend the significance of the miracle. Considering the effort made to find and commune with Him, there was an apparent zeal in their quest, but the shallowness of their commitment was quickly exposed as Jesus responded to their inquiry as He taught in the Synagogue.

> **Jesus answered them and said, Verily, verily, I say unto you, Ye seek me, not because ye saw the miracles, but because ye did eat of the loaves, and were filled. Labour not for the meat which perisheth, but for that meat which endureth unto everlasting life, which the Son of man shall give unto you: for him hath God the Father sealed.**
> **(Joh 6:26-27)**

In spite of their hypocrisy and shallowness, Christ did not shun them or withhold the Word of God from them. He continued to teach them and impart the bread of life to them. This is a lesson to be practiced in our churches today, don't be in such a hurry to dismiss people or withhold the fellowship from those whose background and faith level may be less than stellar. Just as you wouldn't stop administering medication in a hospital simply because sick people came in, you must continue to minister the word when hypocrites enter the church. Besides, it is impossible to know a person's heart. Jesus knew their hearts, that they were wicked and he ministered to them anyway. Perhaps the most important lesson to be gleaned from this episode for the church today is this, <u>doctrine</u> <u>matters</u>!

In the narrative of the evangelist, a reported interruption occurred. Someone asked the question, "**What shall we do, that we might work the works of God?**"

In the opinion of this writer, the interruption was probably not made by one of the outsiders from the way of the sea, but most likely of the Galileans who's Synagogue it was. For one to pose such a question suggests a desire to actually want to accomplish that which God desires. The outsiders clearly were more interested in more earthly interests. Jesus, being the master teacher, used this interruption as an opportunity to take the disciples further and deeper into His doctrine. Even those who were not really inclined to do the works of God need to know the requirements. Often times, many who are doing work in the church confuse such activity as the works of God, when in reality they are just doing busy work at the church. Those who *look high* in their expectations, and hope to enjoy the *glory of God,* must *aim high* in those endeavors, and study to *do the works of God,* works which he requires and will accept, *works of God,* distinguished from the works of worldly men in their worldly pursuits. It is not enough to merely talk the talk but we must also walk the walk. Out of earnest desire, just as the hymnologist and the Philippian jailer inquired, "**what shall I do.......?**" So too did those in the Synagogue that day. Typical of Jesus, he will never allow honest inquiry to go unfilled.

**Jesus answered and said unto them, This is the work of God, that ye believe on him whom he hath sent.
(Joh 6:29)**

As the scripture reminds us and Jesus demonstrates here, he who hungers and thirsts after righteousness shall be filled, but the one work necessary to please God is faith. Christ directs them to one work, which includes all, the one thing needful: that *you must believe,* which trumps all the works of the ceremonial law; the work which is necessary to the acceptance of all the other works, and which produces them, for without faith it is impossible to please God. What follows His response is perhaps the worst case of amnesia ever documented. They have the gall to ask for a sign to verify his credentials as Messiah. These are the same people who feasted upon the multiplied loaves and fishes. Those of Capernaum had witnessed countless miracles, but some they had forgotten all they had seen, or minimized the spiritual importance of the recent events and were seeking another sign. Although there was some legitimacy in there request for another sign. Even Moses gave them signs and wonders to validate his standing as the servant of Jehovah, so their request to Jesus was not without precedent. Having cited the scriptural account of Moses providing manna from heaven as a sign of his divine authority, believing this would prompt Jesus to perform a greater miracle. Christ's response was, "**Moses gave you not that bread from heaven, My Father gives you the true bread.**" Bread which does not perish. **For the bread of God is he which cometh down from heaven, and giveth life unto the world.** Meaning the manna which Moses provided was a mere shadow of the true bread, He himself.

Then said they unto him, Lord, evermore give us this bread. More than likely, a response from one of the Capernaites, indicating an earnest desire for this gift from the Father, which was a sharp contrast from that of the Jews which preceded from the other side of the sea.

❖ **I am the Bread of Life**

> And Jesus said unto them, I am the bread of life: he that cometh to me shall never hunger; and he that believeth on me shall never thirst. But I said unto you, That ye also have seen me, and believe not. All that the Father giveth me shall come to me; and him that cometh to me I will in no wise cast out. For I came down from heaven, not to do mine own will, but the will of him that sent me. And this is the Father's will which hath sent me, that of all which he hath given me I should lose nothing, but should raise it up again at the last day. And this is the will of him that sent me, that every one which seeth the Son, and believeth on him, may have everlasting life: and I will raise him up at the last day. The Jews then murmured at him, because he said, I am the bread which came down from heaven. And they said, Is not this Jesus, the son of Joseph, whose father and mother we know? how is it then that he saith, I came down from heaven? Jesus therefore answered and said unto them, Murmur not among yourselves. No man can come to me, except the Father which hath sent me draw him: and I will raise him up at the last day.
> (Joh 6:35-44)

Clearly, the evangelist is leaving no doubt as to the person and purpose of Jesus, the Christ. As He expounds on his mission and work, the haters abound. The statement, "I am", before Abraham was, "I am", the same "I am" who spoke to Moses from the burning bush, saying, If they ask you who sent you, tell them "I am" sent you. The Jews clearly understood the reference, since it elicited such a negative reaction. So that the scripture readers would not confuse his audience, the language used by the evangelist shifted from referring to them as the "people which stood on the other side of the sea" to the "Jews", the term Jesus always used when referring to His detractors.

"I am that bread of life," alluding to the tree of life in the midst of the garden of Eden, which was to Adam the seal of that part of the covenant, *Do this and live,* of which he might *eat and live.* Christ is the bread of life, for he is the fruit of the *tree of life.* As Jesus continues his teaching of Himself, "**I am that bread**," "**I am the living bread**," "**I am the true bread**," "**that which comes down from heaven**," clearly, a reference to his own divinity. **"He that eateth my flesh, and drinketh my blood, dwelleth in me, and I in him."** Here he is referring to the necessity of receiving, assimilating, and metabolizing the very essence of His doctrine into the fabric of the life of the believer, his listeners, even the sincere found it difficult to fathom. They probably thought he was suggesting to them the practice of cannibalism rather than the requirement of absolute surrender. To those who understood Him correctly, it was too difficult for them.

Many therefore of his disciples, when they had heard *this,* said, This is an hard saying; who can hear it? When Jesus knew in himself that his disciples murmured at it, he said unto them, Doth this offend you? (Joh 6:60-61)

❖ Disciple or Deserter

From that *time* many of his disciples went back, and walked no more with him. Then said Jesus unto the twelve, Will ye also go away?
(Joh 6:66-67)

In his classic work, "My Utmost for His Highest", Oswald Chambers considered this very dilemma when he wrote, "When God, by his Spirit through His Word gives you a clear vision of His will, you must walk in the light of that vision. Mentally disobeying the "heavenly vision" will make you a slave to ideas and views that are completely foreign to Jesus Christ........You can never be the same after the unveiling of a truth. That moment marks you as one who either continues on with even more devotion as a disciple of Jesus Christ, or as one who turns to go back as a deserter." At that point, as the crowd, unable to withstand the hard teaching deserted Him, Jesus turning to his disciples and Simon Peter, responded, "**Lord, to whom shall we go? thou hast the words of eternal life. And we believe and are sure that thou art that Christ, the Son of the living God.**"

CHAPTER 7

Continued Controversy

Then the Jews sought him at the feast, and said, Where is he? And there was much murmuring among the people concerning him: for some said, He is a good man: others said, Nay; but he deceiveth the people. (Joh 7:11-12)

Following the events at Capernaum, more controversy arose. Having sent the twelve ahead to Jerusalem during the feast of tabernacles, Jesus remained in Galilee. **For he would not walk in Jewry,** that is in Judea and Jerusalem, **because the Jews sought to kill him** for curing the impotent man on the Sabbath day. It was not because of fear or cowardice that he avoided it, but in *prudence,* because his hour was not yet come. While in Galilee, He continued to do good, He continued to do ministry. He demonstrated the dictum, "If you can't be with the one you love, love the one you're with." In His words, recorded by St. Matthew, He put it this way, **"But when they persecute you in this city, flee ye into another:**(Matt 10:23)" It is important to remember the divine purpose always take precedence. Never allow personal feelings, pride, or public sentiment to compel you to act in such a manner where God's purpose may be thwarted.

The next dramatic encounter was not the interchange between Jesus and His kinfolks, who were advising Him to go to the feast and perform miracles on the big stage. Their purpose was not unlike many of the other shallow disciples who only wanted to be in the inner circle once he came into power. Much like an entourage of a modern day rock star or professional athlete, as His fame and honor increased, by association, so would theirs. There was nothing dramatic about that because it was always Jesus' intention to go to the feast, he simply wanted to travel under the radar and the big crowd would only hamper His ability to move about unnoticed. *"Shew thyself to the world,"* was their advice, but as the evangelist pointed out, **"for neither did his brethren believe in him."** Clearly, they were not concerned with the best interests of Jesus, only their own glory. They had not bought into His agenda nor supported fully His purpose. Jesus' response to them was, **"My time is not yet come: but your time is alway ready."** So you go ahead without Me, I'm not ready yet.

While the feast was in full swing, Jesus appeared at the temple and in His customary manner, began to teach. The Jews who were aspiring to kill Him were there, but made no effort to apprehend or harm him. Thus proving the axiomatic proverb, **When a man's ways please the LORD, he maketh even his enemies to be at peace with him.** Nevertheless, the encounter did create quite a stir. Some were openly hostile, while some were quite supportive. Nevertheless, they all were wowed, even astonished by his teaching. **And the Jews marvelled, saying, How knoweth this man letters, having never learned?** His knowledge of the law and the Prophets far exceeded that of the Scribes, Priests and Pharisees yet they could not imagine the origin of His knowledge, having never attended their universities or schools of the prophets, or sat under some Rabbi. Christ was perfectly willing to allow them to enquire of the origin of His doctrine, because in doing so, would reveal the inadequacy of their own souls. So he told them, **"My doctrine is not mine, but his that sent me."** The evangelist did not record his sermon, which appeared to be the same message he preached in Galilee and Capernaum, the gospel of the kingdom. It is never inappropriate to preach the gospel, **it is the power of God unto salvation for everyone who believes.** (Rom 1:16) As he preached, he let them know that what He preached was <u>divine</u> in its origin, that those competent to judge it were of a <u>sincere and upright</u> heart and He was <u>not</u> preaching to <u>seek His own glory</u>. The reaction of the hearers prompted a wide variety of responses. Those who wanted to kill Him were even more incensed, some were there that thought he had a devil, but there were some and always are those who truly want to know what the will of God is, because they have every desire to do it, as much as their own power will allow them to. Although most of the onlookers were afraid to speak out for fear of the Jews, others were quite bold, declaring, **"Do the rulers know indeed that this is the very Christ?"** Anyone who honestly examines the evidence and His works in an unbiased manner, will reach that very same conclusion that Jesus of Nazareth is indeed the very Christ. Even the speculation of some the he was the Christ did not prevent others from casting doubt on His identity. By the eighth and final day of the feast, Jesus was still preaching in the temple and the rulers were in an uproar. By then, they had had enough and sent officers into the temple to arrest Him. But the officers made the mistake of listening to Him preach. When they returned to the Rulers and Chief Priests without Jesus, they were asked, **"Why have ye not brought him?"** The officers responded, **"Never man spake like this man."** Even if God can't or won't change a man's heart, he can certainly tie his hands. As the Rulers continued to incite the people against Jesus, Nicodemus, who came to Jesus by night, reminded them of their own laws against lynching a man without due process. When no loophole in the law could be found to justify any action against Him, the dramatic encounter was over and everyone went home.

> **They answered and said unto him, Art thou also of Galilee? Search, and look: for out of Galilee ariseth no prophet. And every man went unto his own house.**
> **(Joh 7:52-53)**

CHAPTER 8

Go and Sin no More

> Jesus went unto the mount of Olives. And early in the morning he came again into the temple, and all the people came unto him; and he sat down, and taught them. And the scribes and Pharisees brought unto him a woman taken in adultery; and when they had set her in the midst, They say unto him, Master, this woman was taken in adultery, in the very act. Now Moses in the law commanded us, that such should be stoned: but what sayest thou?
> (Joh 8:1-5)

Shortly after the feast of tabernacles, perhaps the very next day, the next dramatic encounter occurs. In spite of the abuse He endured at the hands of both the people and the Rulers, Jesus returned to teach. Again a crowd of people showed up. Perhaps these were travelers wanting to hear him preach one more time before they returned to their homes or even some of the locals, the fact remained, they came. Regardless of danger, He still performed His duty. Three things immediately jump out concerning his teaching, the time, the place and his posture.

Having just finished preaching the day before and probably retiring in the countryside that night, he returned early the next morning to preach again. Preach the Word in season and out of season was obviously his practice. While his antagonist lodged in the comfort of their homes, Jesus had to find lodgings elsewhere, because it probably was not safe for him to spend the night in Jerusalem, and none of the locals would have risked going up against the Pharisees and Chief Priests, so prudence and providence dictated that he lodge elsewhere, nonetheless, he still returned early the next day. The place of His return was the temple. In spite of the ruckus, from the feast His duty was there. Not necessarily because the temple was a consecrated place of worship, but most likely because it was the main venue of concourse. The temple is where the largest crowds would congregate, so naturally, If He was going to preach, that would be the place. Thirdly, His posture, He sat down as He taught as one having authority. Also, sitting down here suggested that he was in no hurry and was totally unafraid of the temple storm troopers.

What made the episode a dramatic encounter was the interruption on the part of the scribes and Pharisees who brought a woman to Him who had been caught in the act of adultery. What was interesting about the ordeal was the fact that he same people who on the previous day called him a "deceiver" now approached Him wanting Him to act as judge in an ecclesiastical court case. The evangelist makes it clear concerning the motives of the Jews. At the conclusion of the feast, they had been scrambling trying to find a legal loophole to charge Christ after Nicodemus interrupted their attempt to lynch Him. **They say unto him, Master...**Today, these hypocrites refer to Him as "Master", yet on the previous day, they were attacking his character and good name. Now they are using flatteries to ensnare Him. They declared, "**Now Moses in the law commanded us, that such should be stoned: but what sayest thou?**" It is interesting here, that the man was not brought forth. According to Leviticus 20:10, both the adulterer and the adulteress, should be put to death, but somehow this helpless woman was subdued, but not the man, once again showing their hypocrisy and vindictiveness. What they really had in mind was to trip Jesus up to either openly usurp the law of Moses or dishonor His own practice of forgiveness and grace. He would be branded as either an enemy to Moses or a friend of sinners. Though faced with an apparent dilemma, His initial reaction was as though He did not hear them. He simply wrote on the ground. It is impossible to tell what He wrote, but whatever it was caused a massive shift of attitude. As the mob of men made their approach, those not carrying the young woman, were each carrying stones in anticipation of participating in a public execution. Jesus arose from the dirt and said unto them, "**He that is without sin among you, let him first cast a stone at her.**" After having spoken, he stooped back down and continued to write. Suddenly, the rancor and hatred directed at the women as well as Himself was replaced by shame and contrition.

> **And they which heard *it*, being convicted by *their own* conscience, went out one by one, beginning at the eldest, *even* unto the last: and Jesus was left alone, and the woman standing in the midst.**
> **(Joh 8:9)**

It is the opinion of this writer, that the words written in the dirt may very well have been a list of the names of the illicit sexual partners of the men gathered there or perhaps, even the dollar amounts stolen from the temple treasury, or the bribe prices paid to unscrupulous Roman officials. Whatever it was, the written word and the spoken rebuke, cut them to their core and not a single sole was able to lift a hand against the young woman. This book is about dramatic encounters with Jesus that change the direction of people's lives. Clearly, the direction of the lives of those men who would be executioners was dramatically changed. Where each man once stood, was now a stone. What was intended to be an executioner's weapon was left as a memorial to the saving and convicting power of Christ and a monument to the accusers' shame. The order of their departure is interesting, *beginning at the eldest,* either because they were most guilty, or first aware of the danger they were in of being embarrassed; and if the eldest retreated ingloriously with their tails between their legs, no wonder if the younger follow them. ....**and Jesus was left alone, and the woman standing in the midst.**

The most life changing encounter of the entire episode was not so much the men, but with the young woman. As Jesus lifted up himself, seeing only the young woman, he turned to her and said, **"Woman, where are those thine accusers? hath no man condemned thee?"** Her response was as revealing as the departure of her accusers. She said, **"No man, Lord."** Lordship indicates obeisance to and submission to a higher authority. By calling Him Lord, whatever He would ask her to do, she had already made up in her mind she would do. If Jesus would have asked her to go and dip in the Jordan River seven times, she would have gladly done it. Unlike Naaman, the Syrian general, who balked at the idea, this young woman had a made up mind to obey whatever He would command. Considering what He had just given her, her response was quite reasonable. When a condemned person is given a new life, the one who gives that life deserves to be Lord over that life. Another lesson to be learned from this episode, is the fact that the woman did not make mention of her accusers, who had been shamed into retreat. It would have been easy for her to gloat over their embarrassment, but it is most important for the one who is forgiven to be merciful to others who also need forgiveness. Though she was guilty, her prosecutors vacated the courtroom, the witnesses for the prosecution vanished into the streets and the stood before the judge of the universe who was ready to render a verdict, but the case against her collapse on the grounds that her accusers were more guilty than she and thus unfit to make accusations. But Jesus, unwilling to totally ignore her sin, rendered the sentence. The same sentence had been rendered before when another sinner woman came to Him as He dined at the home of Simon the Pharisee. On the basis of her faith in him, "**thy sins are forgiven, thy faith have saved thee, go......**"(luke7:48). By declaring him "**Lord**", this sinner woman was demonstrating her faith, a faith that saved her natural life. Jesus, the judge, said to her, "**Neither do I condemn thee:**" In effect, he was saying, "your sins are forgiven," proving once again that the Son of Man has power on earth to forgive sin. But it did not end there. This woman, in whose grip, sin had bound profusely, having been delivered from the penalty of sin, still needed deliverance from the power of sin. Forgiveness alone would not be enough to render her capable of breaking from the lust of her flesh. Like many others addicted to sin, she needed treatment. She needed a plan for her recovery; otherwise she would wind up in worse condition than before. So Jesus, the great physician, prescribed for her a treatment plan, "**Go.**" This woman, like all addicts, needed a change of venue. She needed to get away from the people, places and things that were complicit in her past sinful behaviors. Most, if not all secular as well as faith based recovery programs stress the need for detachment from the objects of one's craving. Jesus, the Lover of her soul, knew that although she had been forgiven, and her spirit was willing to obey, her flesh was still weak and in order to obey the second part of the command, "**and sin no more.**" The change in environment was an absolute necessity. To go away from her current situation, was a sign of repentance as she turned away from sin and turned towards God. Also with this command came the implied requirement to change activities. In order to experience God's love, she and all recovering sinners, must do something different. Rather than engaging in hookups with men, join a bible study. Do the things that bring honor to God. The recovering addict must fill his time with positive activities and develop a regimen of spiritual disciplines. You must allow your natural man the opportunity to detoxify of the stuff that made your life a living hell. In the process of obedience to the command to "go", came the power to break free from the hold sin had on her life, which is a lesson all recovering sinners could benefit from.

❖ I Am the Light of the World

It was uncertain whether or not the ensuing encounter occurred the same day the woman in adultery was presented. The evangelist makes no mention of another day and it appears in the text that these were subsequent events. Although the woman's accusers had absconded, there were other scoffers present debating with Jesus as He resumed His preaching at the temple. The second great "I am" statement was declared for their hearing. **"I am the light of the world,"** which is perhaps the most fundamental and important doctrinal statements ever uttered from the mouth of Jesus. Jesus Christ is the light of the world. As one of the rabbis once said, *Light* is the name of the Messiah, as it is written, Dan 2:22, ***And light dwelleth with him***. God is light, and Christ is *the image of the invisible God*. The visible light of the world is the sun, and Christ is the *Sun of righteousness*. One sun enlightens the whole world, so does one Christ, and there needs no more. Christ in calling himself the light expresses the Excellency within himself and the Glory within His personhood. He is saying, what he is to the world, the fountain of light, enlightening every man's path as well as his soul. **"He that followeth me shall not walk in darkness, but shall have the light of life."** The application from this doctrine is, He that follows after me, as a traveler follows the light on a dark night, *shall not walk in darkness*, but *shall have the light of life*. If Christ is to be our light, then, it is our duty to *follow him*, to submit ourselves to his guidance, and in everything take directions from him, in the way that he directs our path. In *12 Steps With Jesus*, Don Williams wrote, "We must separate or be separated from our addictive attachment. This allows us to love in freedom rather than compulsion." The ability to love ourselves, comes as a result of recognizing God's love for us.

When Jesus made the first "I am" statement at the Synagogue at Capernaum, the reaction of the crowd though, was not all negative. Some believed on him but a majority of the disciples walked no more with Him. The second "I am" statement **"I am the light of the world"**, here at the temple garnered an even stronger reaction. This time there were more Pharisees in the audience still smarting from the rebuke of their comrades who persecuted the young woman. Their objection of Christ's doctrine was baseless and showed their hypocrisy and hardness of heart. They said to Him, **"Thou bearest record of thyself; thy record is not true."**

Their objection is not only expected but common among men under self-condemnation, who are lovers of themselves more than lovers of God. What some are all ready to condemn in others, but few are willing to own in themselves. But in this case the objection was unfair because they made that his crime, and attacked the credibility of his doctrine, which in the case of one who introduced a divine revelation was necessary and unavoidable. Moses and all the prophets bore witness of themselves when they presented themselves to be messengers of God. The Pharisees themselves requested self testimony from John the Baptist when they asked, *What sayest thou of thyself?* (John1:22) They overlooked the testimony of all the other witnesses, which corroborated the testimony he bore of himself. Had he only borne record of himself, his testimony had indeed been *dubious* but his doctrine was attested by more than *several* credible *witnesses,* enough to *establish every word* of it. : ... **at the mouth of two witnesses, or at the mouth of three witnesses, shall the matter be established.**(Deut19:15b) Furthermore, the Pharisees and scribes, being experts in the Law and the prophets, knew the scriptures concerning Messiah but here again, whether it is out of ignorance or avarice they have conveniently forgotten them.

Then said Jesus unto them, **When ye have lifted up the Son of man, then shall ye know that I am *he,* and *that* I do nothing of myself; but as my Father hath taught me, I speak these things.** As was the case of the crowd at Capernaum, there were some who believed on Him. Whenever the Word of God goes forth, there will be some who believe, which is why the servants of God must preach the word, in season or out of season.

Concerning the *spiritual liberty* of Christ's disciples, He changed the tone of his preaching with the intent on encouraging *those* Jews *that believed.* Christ, knowing that his doctrine began to work upon some of his hearers, and perceiving that virtue had gone out of him, turned his discourse from the proud Pharisees, and directed himself to those *weak* believers. When he had proclaimed wrath against those that were hardened in unbelief, he then spoke comfort to those few feeble *Jews that believed in him.* **If ye continue in my word,** *then* **are ye my disciples indeed; And ye shall know the truth, and the truth shall make you free.** He that has ears to hear, will always respond to audible voice of the savior. The stiff-necked unbelievers will never hear God speaking to them, they will only hear the voice of their father, the devil. The implication here is that there are some who claim to be disciples, but their actions and attitudes prove otherwise. On the other hand, there are some who indeed are disciples, but because of their infancy and weakness, it may be difficult for the outside world to ascertain, yet He himself knows those who are His own. Although many believers who are disciples indeed do not know everything they should know, yet they will strive to know and must be willing to learn the truths they do not know. The truth which Christ teaches tends to make men free, Justification makes us free from the guilt of sin, by which we were *bound over* to the judgment of God, and *bound under* amazing fears; sanctification makes us free from the bondage of corruption whereby we become more like Jesus day by day. When Christ declared that they needed to be made free, their retort was, **"We are Abraham's seed,"** It is common for a sinking decaying family to boast of the glory and dignity of its ancestors, and to borrow honor from that name to which their actions bring disgrace. Abraham believed God and looked forward to the day when out of his loins all the nations of the earth would be blessed. Much like the woman of Sychar who invoked the name of her ancestors when her sham of a religion was exposed, the Jews clung to their association with Abraham, but their hearts were far from the God of Abraham and had abrogated all rights and privileges due the children of the promise. Once they decided to kill Jesus, the Messiah, they had forfeited all rights as descendants of Abraham. They failed to realize that one's pedigree does not prevent them from going to hell. The Jews declared, **"and were never in bondage to any man: how sayest thou, Ye shall be made free?"** Much like twenty first century America, they were the victims of a revisionist history. Somehow, they managed to forget their four hundred years of bondage in Egypt also their current subjugation under the Romans, but more importantly they were under the bondage of legalism and tradition, yet could not see it. As modern day America is under the bondage of humanism, commercialism and hedonism, she prides herself of liberties and license to live as she pleases much to the point where she does see the decay of her moral fabric nor smell the rot which has putrefied her soul. And like America, the sinfulness of the Jewish culture was so systemic that they had not noticed how far from God they had drifted.

> Jesus answered them, Verily, verily, I say unto you, Whosoever committeth sin is the servant of sin. And the servant abideth not in the house for ever: *but* the Son abideth ever.
> (Joh 8:34-35)

He shows them that, being in a state of bondage, their having a place in the house of God would not entitle them to the inheritance of sons; for *the servant,* though he be in the house for awhile, yet, being but a *servant, abideth not in the house for ever.* Servants get paid, they don't inherit, they are but *temporary,* and not for a *perpetuity; but the son* of the family abideth forever. Jesus Christ in the gospel offers us our freedom; he has authority and power to make us free. To discharge prisoners (as he did for the woman taken in adultery); this he does in justification, by making satisfaction for our guilt (on which the gospel offer is grounded, which is to all a conditional act of indemnity, and to all true believers, upon their faith, an absolute charter of pardon), and for our debts, for which we were foreclosed upon and subject to eviction and forfeiture, Christ, as our surety, or rather the guarantor of our note secured for us the birthright we squandered in the court of divine justice. *For He who knew no sin became sin for us that we might become the righteousness of God in Him.* Under Jewish law, If the first born son of the house, grants an indentured servant his freedom, it is just as binding as if the father had granted that freedom. **So who the Son sets free, is free indeed.**

As Jesus continues teaching, the doctrine of the immortality of believers is presented. It is rendered with the usual solemn preface, **Verily, verily, I say unto you,** which commands both attention and assent, and this is what he says, *If a man keep my sayings, he shall never see death.* Here we have the *true* believer identified as the one that *keeps the sayings* of the Lord Jesus, *ton logon ton emon - my word;* that *word of mine* which I have delivered to you; this we must not only *receive,* but *keep;* not only *have,* but *hold.* We must keep it in mind and memory, keep it in love and affection, so keep it as in nothing to violate it or go contrary to it, keep it *without spot.* To keep it as a trust committed to us, keep in it as our way, keep to it as our rule because it is a lamp unto our feet and a light in our pathway, and in doing so the believer will never see death. The Jews response to this teaching, which should have excited them to the possibility of spiritual immortality, actually rendered them more hostile. Their response to Him, **"Art thou greater than our father Abraham, which is dead? and the prophets are dead: whom makest thou thyself?"** "Who do you think you are Jesus? The greatest Hebrew that ever lived was Abraham, and he is dead, the prophets are all dead, how do you propose to overcome death." (writer's paraphrase) At this point, they are quite incensed, but Jesus responded in the most dramatic fashion, **"Before Abraham was, I am."** Remember the stones the woman's accusers had dropped.

> **Then took they up stones to cast at him: but Jesus hid himself, and went out of the temple, going through the midst of them, and so passed by. (Joh 8:59)**

They were unable to do Him any harm, because His hour had not yet come. In spite of their hatred and rancor, Jesus was able to walk right through the midst of the crowd who clamored for his death. In the mind of the Jews, his statement was blasphemous, but providence would prove every word He spoke was truth.

CHAPTER 9

I must work, while it's Day

> And as *Jesus* passed by, he saw a man which was blind from *his* birth. And his disciples asked him, saying, Master, who did sin, this man, or his parents, that he was born blind?
> (Joh 9:1-2)

The next dramatic encounter occurred as Jesus was fleeing for His life from the religious leaders following the release of the woman taken in adultery. His confrontation with Jews had escalated to the point where they wanted to stone Him. What was interesting to note was the fact that as he was departing the temple area, having just declared Himself as **"the light of the world,"** He spotted a beggar who was born blind and ministered to him. Rather than execute His escape, Jesus sees an opportunity to prove that he truly is the light of the world by doing what only God can do, He performs a healing.

Throughout his gospel, the evangelist is making the case for the deity of Christ, with every miraculous act serving as proof for that very thing. Generally speaking, there are four types of healing, namely; natural healing, where the body, through natural processes and time heals itself; medical healing, where human skill and scientific principals are applied to facilitate healing. Whether it is surgery, where a skilled physician cuts out diseased tissue or even repairs physically damaged tissue facilitating the natural process or the use of chemical, organic or synthetic compounds to alter or effect the natural body chemistry and alleviate certain conditions and promote the formation of healthy cell activity. Then there is emotional or psychological healing which attempts to correct the negative effects of stress, which according to Healthy People 2000, a report from the U.S. Department of Health and Human services, has replaced bacteria as the number one cause of all disease over the last century. Finally, there is divine miraculous healing, where God intervenes in the earth realm and supernaturally injects himself into human history and completely reverses the natural law of entropy, which basically states that all systems lose energy over time and decay. This miraculous divine healing is exactly what Jesus came into this world and preceded to do, which is no problem for Him because He is God incarnate. The miracles He performed were primarily to prove that He, in fact was God.

As we look at the text, we know that this could not be natural healing because the man was born blind. There was no power within him to recover, nor was there any process by which a reversal of his condition could take place. It could not have been medical healing because the discipline of ophthalmology had not been developed. It could not have been psychological because stress did not cause his blindness. It could only be divinely miraculous. The evangelist John makes the point of stressing that there was no natural process, nor medical intervention or psychological shenanigans, only the creative power of almighty God. Just as Jesus has decided to remove Himself from dealing with the religious leaders and wash his hands of the house of Israel, he spots this beggar who was born blind and he heals him.

There are four questions that come to my mind that as I ponder the encounter with this blind man. First of all, what was it that precipitated the healing? Why was the man blind to begin with? What was the manner by which he was healed?, and how did the people react who witnessed the healing? In spite of His own difficult circumstances, Jesus sees a problem. **And as *Jesus* passed by, he saw a man which was blind from *his* birth,** who was apparently there for the purpose of begging for alms. That was a good place to beg because the people who were entering the temple was for the most part, pious, religious folk who were coming to make their sacrifices and do whatever penance their situations deemed necessary. People most likely to be generous were probably coming to and from the temple, so he was in a good spot. Jesus spotted him and performed one of the greatest miracles ever recorded. He not only heals the man of his blindness but he heals his sin sick soul. Like this man, all of us are spiritually blind and unless He sees us we will never be healed because we are incapable of seeing him. That is the way of amazing grace; God sees the sinner and seeks him out.

The purpose of the healing is clearly shown in verse two when the disciples asked Jesus, **"who did sin, this man or his parents that he was born blind?** Which Jesus promptly answers, **"Neither hath this man sinned, nor his parents: but that the works of God should be made manifest in him."** The question might be asked, "why would the disciples ask such a ridiculous question?" The answer is simple, the Jews were taught by the Rabbis that the cause of all disease and calamity was sin, personal sin. According to Dr. Sproul, They even had this ridiculous doctrine of prenatal sin which states that the embryo must have sinned inside the mother's womb causing congenital disease. A medical explanation for congenital blindness is venereal disease.

There was also this antiquated notion of the *pre-existence* of souls, and their *transmigration* from one body to another. Was this man's soul condemned to the dungeon of this blind body to punish it for some great sin committed in another body which it had before animated? This too was a preposterous notion taught by some rabbis. This writer recalls during his youth, one of the girls from his neighborhood contracted syphilis during her pregnancy which went untreated and the child was born blind. Clearly the sin of the mother caused that child's blindness, but that was not the case here. This beggar was chosen to be an instrument of God to manifest in the world His glory; to show the world the magnificent power of God. He was just a miracle waiting to happen. Some theologians compare the driving of Jesus from the spiritually blind Pharisees to the physically blind beggar as an allegory of Jesus abandoning the privileged nation of Israel and bring the glorious gospel to the gentiles.

"I must work the works of him that sent me," said Jesus upon selecting the blind man. What is significant about this text is that there has been some manuscript evidence suggesting that the translation could be rendered, "we must work....", which suggests to the body of Christ that it should be busy working towards changing lives. Christ has identified himself as co-laborers together with His disciples doing the work of ministry. Apart from Him, we can do nothing, but what he has commanded us to do, we must do. What works? Jesus' answer to that question was recorded in the eighteenth verse of chapter four of St. Luke thusly, **"The Spirit of the Lord *is* upon me, because he hath anointed**

me to preach the gospel to the poor; he hath sent me to heal the brokenhearted, to preach deliverance to the captives, and recovering of sight to the blind, to set at liberty them that are bruised, to preach the acceptable year of the Lord." Jesus expects his disciples to minister to the whole man, mind, body and spirit. Reach the lost with the message of salvation found only in the gospel, to meet the physical, emotional as well as the spiritual needs of people with deliberate ministry and the proclamation of the Word of God. In other words, we must get busy doing the work because the harvest is truly plenteous, but the laborers are few.

The church needs to get busy carrying out the Lord's mandate, executing the preaching of the gospel, making disciples, teaching biblical doctrine, exposing sin, and building up the body of Christ. The dramatic encounter with the blind beggar had a purpose far greater than just the restoration of sight to one individual, but as a clarion's call to subsequent generations to get with the program. Notice the phrase in verse four, "….. that sent me," which repeats the message Jesus has been preaching all along, "My meat is to do the will of him that sent me, and to finish his work." It is always about the will of the Father. The Son of Man never set out to exalt Himself or seek glory for Himself, but He came to do what His Father sent Him to do. For Christ, It was always about the Father, for the disciples (including this generation), it must always be about Jesus, for He said, "If I be lifted up, I will draw all men unto me." Also, in the same verse, He states, "while it is day," suggesting a sense of urgency. Stop wasting time. It is not unusual for a ministry or church to spend more time in meetings and planning than actually executing. This writer can recall presenting a proposal to the Executive Pastor regarding a ministry entitled, "Marry Your Baby Mama Ministry". The idea was to identify cohabitating couples, inviting them into the ministry, adopting them, discipling them, helping them become assimilated into the fellowship and giving them a church wedding, at minimal cost to them. Many modern couples forgo marriage thinking an actual wedding is too expensive. The marriage ministry would use recycled dresses and suits and make the events as memorable and beautiful as possible, with the hope that the couple would remain in the church, raise their families in the fear of the Lord, according to biblical precepts and let the chips fall where they may. Recently, an actual couple decided to have a marriage ceremony after the morning worship service. It appeared to be very impromptu, but the entire congregation helped them celebrate their commitment to one another. This was exactly the type of moment the *Marry Your Baby Mama* ministry was supposed to create. It has been over two years since the proposal, and the recent wedding served as proof that a deliberate effort to minister in this area would be quite fruitful, yet no mention or action. It could not be determined if the Executive Pastor ever brought the proposal up in one of her bi-weekly women's ministry meetings or not. Churches spend a lot of time planning and very little time actually doing the work.

The reason Jesus stressed such a sense of urgency is given in the same verse, **"the night cometh: when no man can work."** Jesus knew that his time on earth was limited and no time should be wasted. In spite of the fact that there was a mob ready to stone Him, Jesus sees a man with a problem, while totally disregarding his own precarious situation, He stops and heals the man. Jesus is reminding the church here that windows of opportunity close quickly and must be taken advantage of. If ever anyone had a reason to not stop but keep going it was Jesus, yet he recognized in this dramatic encounter a divine opportunity to glorify His Father. **"As long as I am in the world, I am the light of the world."** It is so unfortunate that many in the body of Christ choose to run from God or delay serving Him many years before they relent and commence doing what they knew in their hearts they were called to do years sooner. The idea of souls lost because a slothful servant was too lazy to share the good news with sinners whose hearts God had prepared, and opportunities given, is a sobering thought. Jesus knew that within a few short weeks, He would no longer be in the world so He knew he had to act now. He made a business of that which was His business. His business was to bring the light of the gospel into the world so that men might be saved.

When he had thus spoken, he spat on the ground, and made clay of the spittle, and he anointed the eyes of the blind man with the clay. Many theologians and preachers have speculated why He chose to use the dust of the earth and saliva as instruments of healing. It has been said that he used clay to signify the fact that man came from the dust of the earth. Others speculated that the clay covering his eyes represented sin that conceals the light of grace from entering a man's heart. It is the opinion of this writer that Jesus chose to use spit and dirt because he chose to use spit and dirt. Why not? One can only speculate why he chose to do it that way. **And said unto him, "Go, wash in the**

pool of Siloam," (which is by interpretation, Sent.) He went his way therefore, and washed, and came seeing.** Accepting the speculation about the use of the clay, there is no speculation concerning the use of the pool of Siloam. The pool of Siloam was a little pond located inside the wall near the east gate. There was a spring called the Gihon Spring, or the Virgins' Font, up on the temple mount. In order to assure water in the city in the event of a siege, According to Josephus, Hezekiah had built an aqueduct, a tunnel running the water from the spring up on the hill where the temple was right down into the pool of Siloam so there would always be a water supply in the event of a siege. The Old Testament name for that pool was called "Shiloah," which now has been rendered in the Greek Siloam and it meant "Sent." From the temple hill the water was sent and this was the sent water. Josephus described it as "sweet" waters. The temple hill was a place where God was represented so naturally Siloam represented that which was sent from God, represented Him of His blessings. And so Jesus is saying go wash in Siloam, the water sent by God, it will cleanse your eyes. Without any ado, the man simply wandered away to Siloam, complied with the command of Jesus and washed the clay from his eyes, seeing. It is amazing how Jesus meets people where they are and gives them what they need. In all these dramatic encounters, Jesus does not wait for the people to go and straighten themselves out; he meets them at the point of their need. He met the Samaritan woman at the very well which was a monument to her shame, giving her the living water; he met the five thousand famished people on the hillside where they hungered and gave them the bread of life; He gave the impotent man the power to carry the very thing that once carried him; He exposed the hypocrisy of the Jews right in the temple where they carried out their vain and empty worship; He gave deliverance to the adulteress while she still bore the stench of her illicit lover. He worked the work where and when it was needed.

Later that day, the previously blind man, after having been expelled from the synagogue had another encounter with Jesus. Jesus knew his work was undone. Having healed the man of physical blindness, there remained the unfinished business of the soul, so Jesus sought him out and found him, to test his faith, asked him, **"Dost thou believe on the Son of God?"** In other words, the question was, "Do you believe in the promises of Messiah?" Word of his bold witness in the Synagogue had obviously been relayed to Jesus, either by revelation or eyewitness, who was determined to complete that which he had already begun and reward him as he does all who suffer for righteousness sake. Jesus Christ will be sure to stand by his witnesses, and own those that own him and his truth and ways. **He answered and said, Who is he, Lord, that I might believe on him? And Jesus said unto him, Thou hast both seen him, and it is he that talketh with thee.** Like any sane person who had a dramatic encounter with Jesus and received from Him the gift of God, he responded in the most appropriate manner imaginable. **And he said, Lord, I believe.** For whosoever shall call upon the name of the Lord, shall be saved. By proclaiming Jesus as Lord indicated a truly grateful servant who would be entitled to every spiritual blessing available from heaven, but so that there would be no possibility of misreading the extent of his gratitude, **And he worshipped him.** Chuck Swindoll once called worship man's response to God's redemption. Unlike the vain, empty worship of the Pharisees, this was worship not only in spirit, but also in truth.

And Jesus said, For judgment I am come into this world, that they which see not might see; and that they which see might be made blind. And *some* of the Pharisees which were with him heard these words, and said unto him, Are we blind also? Jesus said unto them, If ye were blind, ye should have no sin: but now ye say, We see; therefore your sin remaineth. (Joh 9:39-41)

CHAPTER 10

I am the Good Shepherd

> Verily, verily, I say unto you, He that entereth not by the door into the sheepfold, but climbeth up some other way, the same is a thief and a robber. But he that entereth in by the door is the shepherd of the sheep. To him the porter openeth; and the sheep hear his voice: and he calleth his own sheep by name, and leadeth them out. And when he putteth forth his own sheep, he goeth before them, and the sheep follow him: for they know his voice. And a stranger will they not follow, but will flee from him: for they know not the voice of strangers. (Joh 10:1-5)

The next dramatic encounter recorded by the evangelist does not occur with his disciples but with his nemesis, the Pharisees. Not every dramatic encounter will be with those who find favor with Christ. There will always be encounters with foes as well. The Pharisees had prided themselves as those in the know. They paraded themselves around with such pompous arrogance they were sickening. They bolstered their opposition to Christ with this principle, that they were the *pastors of the church,* and that Jesus, having no affiliation with them, was an intruder and an impostor, and therefore the people were bound in duty to side with *them,* against *him.* In opposition to this, Christ describes here who the false shepherds were, as well as the authentic, leaving them to see the truth for themselves. He begins His discourse in a dramatic and serious fashion, "**Verily, verily,**" amen, amen, denoting the certainty and weight of what is being said. As typical of Jesus, he uses the common to illustrate the divine. The husbandry of sheep was a staple of the culture, so to use sheep in the object lesson was another master stroke on His part. To really understand the similitude, one must first explore Ezekiel chapter thirty-four, which deals exclusively with God's chastisement of the shepherds of Israel where the prophet is ordered to *prophesy against the shepherds of Israel*; the princes and magistrates, the priests and Levites, the Sanhedrin or council of state, or anyone responsible for the administration of God's heritage. Although God called them shepherds, they were in essence His under-shepherds responsible to Him, the great Shepherd of Israel.

Give ear, O Shepherd of Israel, thou that leadest Joseph like a flock; thou that dwellest *between* the cherubims, shine forth. (Psa 80:1)

In his charge to the Shepherds of Israel, **Ezekiel** exposed their greed and selfish ambition. Their practice of enriching themselves at the expense of God's people was deplorable and justified the most severe condemnation. **"Woe *be* to the shepherds of Israel that do feed themselves! should not the shepherds feed the flocks?"** Ezekiel's diatribe is almost identical to the condemning speech of Jesus recorded in the twenty third chapter of the Gospel of St. Mathew verse fourteen, **"Woe unto you, scribes and Pharisees, hypocrites! for ye devour widows' houses, and for a pretence make long prayer: therefore ye shall receive the greater damnation."** Jesus' most blunt language was always directed towards the scribes and Pharisees, the de-facto, shepherds of Israel who violated the very principle Ezekiel outlined in his prophecy many centuries before. Much like the modern day prosperity preachers who profane the ministry of Jesus Christ with the lavish lifestyles and extravagant behaviors such as those depicted on the very popular reality TV show "The Preachers of L.A." and the antics of the Archbishop of Atlanta who purchased a two million dollar mansion with church funds, these shepherds lifestyles bring into question the sincerity of their walk of faith. Their opulence could easily add to the hopelessness of their parishioners facing foreclosure and other economic challenges. Having to watch your pastor flaunt his wealth while you live in squalor must be heartbreaking for some. Nevertheless, the scriptures clearly teach that the "workman is worthy of his hire", and that those who are ministered to, have a responsibility to reward those who minister to them. At the same time, the ministers have a responsibility to not become stumbling blocks to those in their charge. The damage done by those shepherds caught in sexual misconduct have devastated the credibility of the church.

"He who does not enter into the sheepfold by the door, but going up by another way, that one is a thief and a robber," Jesus making a reference to those whose entrance into ministry was of their own choosing rather than a call of God. Those unbelieving priest (and preachers) who only through natural bloodline became ministers of God's heritage without the benefit of even an unction to serve. Based solely on family ties being Levites (because daddy and granddaddy were preachers), Jesus evokes His wrath upon these brigands. He compares them to thieves and robbers, in that they usurp the cause of God by both stealth and overt abuse. **"I am the door,"** Indicating the necessity of salvation as the qualification of being a shepherd. The unsaved preacher is as deadly today as he was in Jesus' day, causing shipwreck the faith of many with duplicitous lifestyles and cancerous doctrine.

Not much has changed since the days of Hophni and Phinehas, the sons of Eli (1 Samuel chapter 2), described there as, "sons of Belial (the devil), who knew not the Lord." These two so called men of God profaned the priest's office with their hedonism and debauchery while serving in the temple. Many false preachers of our day act like pimps in the pulpit, treating their congregants as whores in a stable, exploiting them and enriching themselves. It is easy to criticize the actions of those such as the Preachers of L.A. for their brazen lifestyles even in the presence of sound doctrine and biblical effectiveness. It is certainly unwise for them to expose their weaknesses and imperfections to open scrutiny. It may be more prudent to cover one's nakedness than expose it to open shame and run the risk of alienating the faithful and running away those who may be seeking the truth. On the other hand, perhaps it is the very appearance of prosperity in a righteous manner which can compete with the world system and its propensity for unrighteous mammon. This writer has re-thought his initial impression of these preachers after having heard their message. To categorize them with the likes of Hophni and Phinehas, may be unfair. Their worldliness, being so well documented and publicized as well as admitting to their personal weaknesses and failures has not occurred in secret, nor has the regret and repentance for their failures. Nevertheless, it would still be more prudent to deal with one's moral failures and weaknesses along with personal prosperity in a more private manner. Boasting of one's personal prowess brings no glory to God and casts a pall on the cause of Christ. Just as insidious as the pimps in today's pulpits are the complacent and the complicit. Such were the actions of the southern preachers who criticized Dr. Martin Luther King Jr. during his day, as he languished in a Birmingham Alabama jail for merely standing up for righteousness and fulfilling the law of Christ. In his 1963 Letter From a Birmingham Jail, Dr. King had responded to criticism from a group of clergymen who called his participation in the Birmingham movement "meddling and counter-productive." The Clerics had suggested to Dr. King that he should cease and desist from his direct involvement into the affairs of city of Birmingham. The letter was an itemized response to the accusations made against him. One statement that stuck out to this writer was directed mainly to the white clergy,

> When I was suddenly catapulted into the leadership of the bus protest in Montgomery, Alabama, a few years ago, I felt we would be supported by the white church. I felt that the white ministers, priests and rabbis of the South would be among our strongest allies. Instead, some have been outright opponents, refusing to understand the freedom movement and misrepresenting its leaders; all too many others have been more cautious than courageous and have remained silent behind the anesthetizing security of stained glass windows.

> In spite of my shattered dreams, I came to Birmingham with the hope that the white religious leadership of this community would see the justice of our cause and, with deep moral concern, would serve as the channel through which our just grievances could reach the power structure. I had hoped that each of you would understand. But again I have been disappointed.
> –M.L.K, 1963

Just as the pastors of Israel were guilty of exploiting the flock of God in Ezekiel's day and some prosperity preachers are guilty of exploiting the flock in our day, the pastors of Dr. King's day were equally complicit in their day by standing by and allowing others to assail and oppress God's people and turning a blind eye to the injustice. Rather than upset the status quo and side with justice and freedom, the pastors of America's south retreated behind their varnished pulpits, never challenging the gospel of hate propagated by so many in their congregations. Had the sin of racism been preached alongside the sin of idolatry, perhaps it would have taken less than three hundred years for the black man to taste freedom. Had the sin of segregation been preached along with the sins of murder and mayhem, countless lynchings and bombings could have been averted. For those who call upon the name of the Lord and identify themselves as Christian to continue to do the things that dishonor God and give a black eye to the cause of Christ is a travesty. But for those who have been charged with the task of feeding the flock of God, of making disciples and preaching the gospel, they are also charged with the task of preaching repentance, providing reproof, giving instruction in righteousness and correct living. To be negligent in any of these areas would leave one to doubt if they truly believed any of it. Were they truly shepherds of God or just hirelings that went with the program and collected their pay-checks? Were they willing to sacrifice for their sheep? Were they prepared to withstand some criticism and endure hardship for the cause of Christ? Were they willing to lay down their lives for their sheep? At least the "Preachers of L.A." make no pretense of their true motives, running the risk of offending some to gain others and not bother hiding behind a veneer of piety as did the "Preachers of the South during Dr. King's day.

One could easily understand Dr. King's disappointment with the preachers of his day, both black and white, and could speculate upon the disappointment he might have with the "Preachers of L.A." and such. But for today's black preachers to allow the "Gay Rights crowd to steal the civil rights banner and equate the sin of sodomy with the race is an outrage of which this writer is certain Dr. King would have an issue with. While King's martyrdom was a testimony to his commitment to God and the plan of God, the silence of his critics and others in decrying injustice was a testimony to theirs as well as the silence of the black preachers of our day. They have been silent in defending the sanctity of marriage, human life and morality in public policy. It is important to take a public stand on the issues of our day. Like the "Good Shepherd", a preacher's actions will prove whose he is, for his silence is often more eloquent than his speech and his silence proves he is either an evil accomplice or a complacent coward. The reluctance of many preachers today to condemn sin in all its forms from their pulpits out of fear of offending some is sickening. Like the lukewarm church at Laodicea in the Book of Revelation, it makes you want to "puke". I am not advocating treating those who practice the gay lifestyle in an ungodly and unloving manner. They too have been deceived into believing that the whole of their identity is wrapped up in their sin nature. They wrongly believe that they were born gay when in reality they were simply born sinners like all of us, but their sin nature happens to manifest itself sexually. God made all of us all social as well as sexual creatures so that we will be able to obey His command to be fruitful and multiply and replenish the earth. The sex drive was God's idea. It is as basic as the need to eat and sleep. God designed human sexuality to be not only functional but pleasurable. Unlike the other creatures of the earth whose sexual activity is limited solely for the act of sustaining the species, we humans have the ability to engage in sex purely for pleasure if we choose to do so. However, it is in the marriage bed that this gift from God is to be enjoyed. The autonomic nature of sexuality lends itself to abuse and license. The innate physical pleasure of sex can be enjoyed by anyone under almost any circumstance. The pleasure sensors in the brain which produce arousal are completely independent of rational thought and an orgasm can be achieved simply by physical manipulation of sensory tissue. The pleasure of an orgasm will be experienced with or without a partner or with feelings for that partner. It is in marriage where the highest order of human companionship is achieved because God designed it that way. For the shepherds of our society to cast aside divine order and promote alternative lifestyles is flirting with disaster of epic proportions.

In this very public chastisement of the Pharisees, where Jesus continues to contrast the good shepherd from the false, He points out that the Good Shepherd will sacrifice himself for his sheep. His continued use of the phrase "**I am**" clearly points to His deity and equality with God the father and elicits the most hostile of reactions from the non-believing Jews to the point of total rejection. What makes this encounter so dramatic is the fact that it marks the end of the public ministry of Jesus and precipitates the countdown to glory. No further direct attempt to convince the unbelievers will be made. His ministry efforts will be concentrated upon those who have already professed faith in him and seek to know the truth. His primary activity from this point forward would be to prove that He was truly the "Good Shepherd", to take care of His own sheep and to glorify His Father.

> Therefore doth my Father love me, because I lay down my life, that I might take it again. No man taketh it from me, but I lay it down of myself. I have power to lay it down, and I have power to take it again. This commandment have I received of my Father. (Joh 10:17-18)

It is the responsibility of the sheep to pay attention to the voice of their own shepherd. One of the biggest hindrances to spiritual growth in the church is the tendency of many to church hop. Church hopping is the practice of going from church to church grazing from many different tables. Even if there are no major doctrinal differences from one preacher to the next, being exposed to an accumulation of minor differences can only add to the erosion of discernment and the creation of dullness of hearing. Experiencing differing worship styles and hearing other God sent preachers in and of itself is not harmful. Nevertheless, discernment is still the order of the day. One must always keep their spiritual antennae in array. In the words of Hank Hannagraf, the "Bible Answer-Man", "one must become so familiar with the truth, when the counterfeit pops up, you will know it immediately."

CHAPTER 11

Loose That Man

> Now a certain *man* was sick, *named* Lazarus, of Bethany, the town of Mary and her sister Martha.   (Joh 11:1)

It is in the town of Bethany that the next dramatic encounter will occur. Bethany was the home of Mary, Martha and their brother Lazarus. Bethany was about two miles southeast of Jerusalem. It was apparently customary for Jesus to abide with them whenever he was in the area. They certainly knew where he was because they sent word to him when Lazarus became gravely ill and unlike the unbelieving Jews who sought to kill him and could not find him, Mary and Martha knew exactly where he was. What was always interesting was this; those that believed on Him could always find Him, yet He was always out of reach of those who believed not. The interesting thought in the communiqué was the wording chose. **"Lord, behold, he whom thou lovest is sick."** In the minds of the sisters, it was a foregone conclusion that Jesus could and would do something although they never intimated what they thought He should do. Their faith in Jesus grew out of the love that Jesus had for them. They loved Jesus because He first loved them. Their faith in Jesus obviously transcended his works because it was Mary, who anointed the Lord with ointment and wiped his feet with her hair, as acts of worship and honor to the person of Christ. Never missing an opportunity to bring glory to His Father, Jesus would use the sickness of Lazarus for this very purpose. He said, **"This sickness is not unto death, but for the glory of God, that the Son of God might be glorified thereby"**. It is important for believers to remember that in the midst of human suffering, there is always a divine purpose that at the present time may not understood, but in due season, will be revealed and his glory manifested. Also important for the believers to understand is that the sickness inherent in all natural men is not unto death because God has given mankind a remedy for that sickness, His son Jesus. What began as an embarrassing moment at a wedding, turned into an opportunity to glorify God, a nobleman's sick child, an impotent man at a sheep pool, a man born blind, a hillside with five thousand hungry people, a stormy night at sea, all turned into other opportunities to glorify God, this encounter at Bethany would prove to be another such incident as is true of all the miracles performed by Jesus, they are all for the purpose of bringing glory to God. Having to watch their brother waste away had to be difficult for Mary and Martha, but Jesus, in spite of His love for them allowed them to endure this heartache. He knew that the glory to be revealed would far exceed their suffering at that present time and for the saints, this present age.

Delaying his departure to Bethany for two days was not an indication of callous disregard to the plight of his loved ones. Jesus was just setting the stage for perhaps, the greatest encounter of all. When the decision to depart for Judea was made, the disciples were very wary of making the journey because the Jews had sought to kill Jesus during the last trip. **His disciples say unto him, "Master, the Jews of late sought to stone thee; and goest thou thither again?"** Clearly, the disciples failed to see the big picture. But He reminded them of the need of urgency in carrying out the mission. There is always a tendency to waste valuable time in the execution of God's plan in the earth. Once the mission parameters are laid out and marching orders given, the believers must resist the temptation to dawdle but to act with purpose and fortitude. When Jesus, the Light of the World is leading the way, there is never a reason to waver in one's quest to serve God or to do His will. As they went along the way, other ministry and teaching opportunities presented themselves, which points out another great truth. In the process of doing "the great thing", do not neglect the opportunities to do the small positive things along the way. It was on this trip back to Bethany that Jesus brought about the conversion of Zaccheus, the healing of blind Bartimaeus the son of Timaeus, the object lesson of the fig tree, all the while preparing for His triumphal entry into Jerusalem.

By the time of His arrival, Lazarus had been dead four days. Obviously, his death must have occurred at about the time of the news of his sickness arrived to Jesus. After the two day delay and subsequent trip, it was now the fourth day of his entombment, assuming the Jewish custom of burying the dead on the day of death was followed. Also the body of Lazarus was in the state of advanced decomposition. News of Jesus' arrival preceded Him and Martha went out to meet Him. In an amazing show of faith in the presence of an apparent dim view of the Awesomeness of God, she said, **"Lord, if thou hadst been here, my brother had not died."** Martha never doubted the ability or willingness of Jesus to heal her brother in his sickness. In spite of her great faith, her mind was incapable of apprehending the possibilities, for she said, **"But I know, that even now, whatsoever thou wilt ask of God, God will give** *it* **thee."** This was perhaps the greatest acknowledgement of faith displayed in all of scripture. Her view of God was quite accurate, it was astounding in fact yet it displayed some minute flaws. Jesus said to her, **"thy brother shall rise again."** Martha saith unto him, **"I know that he shall rise again in the resurrection at the last day."** In addition to her commendable faith, Martha also showed a remarkably accurate view of the big picture of God. Her theology and eschatology far exceeded that of the Pharisees and especially that of the Sadducees and was about to get her rewarded in a manner never imagined. An accurate view of God is an absolute necessity for spiritual life. Regarding the need to view God accurately, Tozer wrote, "A right conception of God is basic not only to systematic theology but to practical Christian living as well. I believe there is scarcely an error in doctrine or a failure in applying Christian ethics that cannot be traced finally to imperfect and ignoble thoughts about God." Martha's thoughts of God and His Christ were nobler than anyone on record. Having developed an intimacy with God few could have attained being personally tutored by Jesus Himself, her doctrine was impeccable. Jesus never wasted teachable moments with his disciples and Martha alone with her sister Mary took advantage of the many availed to them. Jesus' response to her declaration of faith and sound doctrine must have astonished her. Knowing her brother Lazarus' faith and love for Jesus, gave her much confidence in his eternal destiny, with assurance that he would be resurrected on the last day, but she was about to get an intrusive word. Jesus said to her, **"I am the resurrection, and the life: he that believeth in me, though he were dead, yet shall he live: And whosoever liveth and believeth in me shall never die."** This was another of the "I am" statements made by Jesus furthering his claim to deity. So that there would be no illusions as to what was about to take place, Jesus asked her to make a personal assessment of the revelatory bombshell he had just dropped on her. **"Believest thou this?"** You called me Lord, do you believe that I am Lord even over death? Amazingly, her response was almost identical to the response Peter had a few days earlier when Jesus asked him, **"who do men say that I am?"** She saith unto him, **"Yea, Lord: I believe that thou art the Christ, the Son of God, which should come into the world."** And immediately, she responded the way all true believers who come into revelation knowledge of Jesus as the Christ. She went to tell the person or persons she loves the most, which in this case was her sister Mary, who wasted no time coming to where Jesus was. Just as Andrew did when he found the Lord, he went to tell his brother Peter, just as Philip went and found Nathanael. This is the pattern the church has always followed and should follow today, when you find Jesus for yourself, go and tell someone you love where you found him that they too may find Him for themselves. Mary, upon seeing the Master had the same response as her sister, she fell at his feet and worshipped and having the same faith in the power of Christ, she too said, **"Lord, if thou hadst been here, my brother had not died."** Although these two sisters grieved over the loss of their brother to death, they were quite content with the knowledge that their brother knew and loved the Lord and were assured of his eternal salvation. They were also certain of the love that Jesus had for them and their deceased brother, but their grief was real. Jesus, recognizing what he had put them through for the purpose of glorifying the Father would not allow their faith, love and sacrifice go unrewarded. His very presence brought them solace as he shared with them the pain of their apparent loss. He too was overcome with grief but not over the death of Lazarus, but in empathy over the pain of Mary and Martha along with their friends. The sisters, as well as the believing Jews who were present all felt that If Jesus had gotten there in time, Lazarus would have been healed. In their minds, it was too late. Their only consolation was the resurrection, which would have sufficed them.

"Where have you laid him?" Jesus asked. Directing him to the tomb, made out of a cave with a stone laid over the opening, much like the one Jesus himself would be borrowing in a few days. The grave, which according to the writer of Proverbs can never be satisfied, serves as the final resting place of a person's physical remains. It is also symbolic of the end of all the hopes and dreams a person may have had in this life, yet it is about to meet its match. Whatever plans the sisters may have made with their brother were seemingly all to naught because here they stood at the gravesite. According to Jewish tradition, the body was wrapped in "linen clothes," and the face bound about with a napkin. As his body was being wrapped in grave-clothes, so too were their hopes, their dreams and their aspirations for Lazarus. But when Jesus made the next request of them, they were taken aback. Jesus said, "**Take ye away the stone.**" Martha's response was quite reasonable considering the advanced state of corruption of the now four day old corpse. **"Lord, by this time he stinketh:"** When human tragedy is allowed to run its course, there is the inevitable feeling of giving up. In her mind, it was too late, even for Jesus. But the place where we give up on the possibilities of man is the place where God is allowed to step in. Human effort in spiritual things acts as a hindrance to the move of God, but there are times when God wants men to act. This was one of those times, as Martha was reminded. "**Said I not unto thee, that, if thou wouldest believe, thou shouldest see the glory of God?**" In order to see the glory of God, men must act in obedience to His commands. **Then they took away the stone *from the place* where the dead was laid. And Jesus lifted up his eyes, and said, "Father, I thank thee thou hast heard me. And I knew that thou hearest me always; but because of the people which stand by I said it, that they may believe that thou hast sent me.**" Because the fullness of the power of God resided in Jesus, it was not necessary for him to pray to the Father to bring about the resurrection of Lazarus, but for the benefit of the saints to see the pattern to be modeled in practice of our faith, but also for the benefit of the witness of those who believed on Him and would carry on the work after His departure. Henry wrote, "Elijah and Elisha raised the dead, as servants, by *entreaty;* but Christ, as a Son, by *authority*, having life in himself, and the power to quicken whom he would", as he was about to display at the tomb of his friend. **"Lazarus, come forth,"** cried Jesus with a loud voice. It has been said, that if Jesus had not called Lazarus by name, the entire cemetery would have been emptied. Just as the people had obeyed Jesus' command to move the stone away, the mortal remains of Lazarus were compelled to obey His command and reanimate and come forth out of the tomb, still bound hand and foot in his graveclothes. Because the odor of death and decay were still on the graveclothes, Jesus commanded them to **"Loose him, and let him go."** The graveclothes symbolize the nature of the old man, subject to corruption and decay. The resurrection of Lazarus was symbolic of the new birth in that what was once physically dead was quickened by the spirit of God and made alive. So upon the new birth, it is necessary for the new man to separate himself from every vestige of the old life and get loosed from the burdens of the past. Because he was completely bound, it was going to take some help from the community of believers to assist in the unraveling of the new man from the old life, which is the duty of the church. Even though the graveclothes stunk, it was needful for those who love the Lord to not allow the discomfort of the task to dissuade them from doing it, and not grow weary in well doing. Unlike the resurrection of the daughter of Jairus and the son of the widow of Nain, both of whom had died and were made alive the same day, this miracle was the most glorious yet in that it was done in the face of total corruption of the man Lazarus and the total rejection of the Jewish nation. It also validated all the previous claims Jesus. Anyone who ever doubted his claim to be the fountain of "**living water**" must rethink their doubt. His claim to be "the **bread of life**", could never again be questioned. His claim to be the eternal "**I am**", could never again be mocked. His claim to be "**the light of the world**," now had more brilliance than ever. His claim to be "**the door**" of salvation had been completely vindicated as well as His claim to be the "**Good Shepherd.**" By resurrecting a completely decomposed body after four days proved not only that he was "**the Resurrection and the Life**," but he was Lord of not only the living but also the dead, thus making Him fit to be the judge of both. Not only did the raising of Lazarus from the dead bring glory to God by validating the claims of Jesus' deity, but it also strengthened the faith of the believers. **Then many of the Jews which came to Mary, and had seen the things which Jesus did, believed on him.** Mary and Martha already had much faith, but after this, they had mighty faith. In addition to strengthening the faith of the believers, the raising of Lazarus glorified God because it precipitated the countdown to the cross. From this point on, the plotting to end His life would intensify and the forces of darkness would continue to carry out their devilish, yet unbeknownst to them, divine plan.

But some of them went their ways to the Pharisees, and told them what things Jesus had done. Then gathered the chief priests and the Pharisees a council, and said, What do we? for this man doeth many miracles. If we let him thus alone, all *men* will believe on him: and the Romans shall come and take away both our place and nation. (Joh 11:46-48)

CHAPTER 12

Dramatic Conflict

> Then saith one of his disciples, Judas Iscariot, Simon's *son*, which should betray him, Why was not this ointment sold for three hundred pence, and given to the poor? This he said, not that he cared for the poor; but because he was a thief, and had the bag, and bare what was put therein. (Joh 12:4-6)

The raising of Lazarus from the dead brought about a mixture of various responses from those who were affected by and were made aware of this dramatic event. The emotions ranged from unabashed love to outright hostility. The people who loved Him loved Him the more and the people who hated Him grew even more intense in their hatred. Shortly After this, a group of the disciples decided to have an appreciation dinner for Jesus. Probably more interesting than the timing was its setting. Apparently, it took place In Bethany the village of Lazarus, at the home of Simon the leper. **There they made him a supper;** Obviously, Simon had been healed of his leprosy because there would not have been feast at his home if he was still infected. In fact, if he was still infected with leprosy, the home they were in probably would have been burned to the ground. Furthermore, Simon was probably healed by Jesus himself, who was the only known cure for leprosy. The feast was replete with not only the true believers, but also some of His haters. At this time, the public ministry of Jesus was completely shut down following the Jewish rejection, and his only interest at this time was building up the faith of His disciples; encouraging them, preparing them, teaching more about Himself that they will be able to carry out the mission once He left this earth. He knew that he only had a short time to be with them and wanted to waste none of it. Possibly sensing for themselves the scarcity of time, the disciples wanted to show Jesus how much they appreciated him so they put together this potluck dinner. And just as one might expect, **Martha served.** It was just like Martha, "Miss Congeniality", looking out for the needs of others. Her love for Jesus showed in very practical ways. She was not one of those believers that was so "heavenly minded" they are of no earthly good. She was always very practical. No church can function properly without at least one Martha. Any pastor serious about growing a ministry will spend his first few weeks in a new pastorate trying to identify someone in the congregation who possesses the spirit of Martha, that servant's spirit interested only in serving the needs of others and not worrying about personal glory and recognition. Concerning the servant's spirit Jesus said, "He that would be chiefest among you, let him be your servant." This was not even Martha's house, but we find her doing what she does, serving others and doing what needs to be done.

It was customary in that day, that the men would be seated while the women congregated along the periphery. More than likely, Jesus would have been at the head of the table with the twelve seated around it in their normal pecking order, **but Lazarus was one of them that sat at the table with him.** This confirms that this was not in the home of Lazarus, but another, in this case Simon. Interestingly, these two men, Simon the ex-leper and Lazarus the ex-deadman, two crown jewels of the ministry of Christ were seated together for all to see, for all to recognize the power and glory of Christ, in the face of the most hostile of opposition yet here they were celebrating their Lord and Christ. All of a sudden, out of the blue, **then took Mary a pound of ointment of spikenard, very costly, and anointed the feet of Jesus, and wiped his feet with her hair.** In a spontaneous display of love and compassion, Mary broke an alabaster box of ointment and poured it out on Jesus' head and it rolled down all the way to his feet. This ointment made of spikenard was very expensive having been imported from the Far East. It was one of those items, people kept on display but never used. This box was undoubtedly Mary's most prized possession, but she chose to expend on Jesus. In an unashamed display of love and adoration, she not only poured it out on his head, but she wiped off the residue which dripped to his feet with her hair. A Jewish woman would never let her hair down in the presence of men, but Mary did not care what anyone thought, she simply displayed the total love for

Jesus that she felt. Amazingly, this range of emotions was brought about as a result of the raising of Lazarus from the dead. Martha's congeniality and Mary's compassion were on full display but another emotion was about to rear its head and one not quite as noble as that displayed by the sisters. **Then saith one of his disciples, Judas Iscariot, Simon's *son*, which should betray him.** In the midst of this jubilant crowd, a mixture of disciples, friends, curious onlookers and hostile Jews, was also Judas, one of the twelve. Having blended into the very fabric of the life of Jesus, Judas managed to portray himself as a pious believer, but the unabashed, unrehearsed act of love and compassion committed by Mary, revealed the true heart of Judas, one of pure covetousness. Mary's compassion revealed Judas's selfishness, greed and covetousness. **"Why was not this ointment sold for three hundred pence, and given to the poor?"** The Evangelist John confirmed Judas' true motives when he wrote in his gospel, **"This he said, not that he cared for the poor; but because he was a thief, and had the bag, and bare what was put therein."** Judas was probably a very impressive individual. Much like the Pharisees, he could talk a very good game, but his motives were never pure. Judas wanted to be close to Jesus as long as he thought that he could get something out of the deal. That's probably why he accepted the role as treasurer, so that he could embezzle the money. When he saw that box of ointment pouring out, he could not contain himself; he could only see his booty dripping away. His sway over the other disciples was obvious because many of them were in agreement with his assessment of the extravagance of Mary's act. In St. Matthew's account of this encounter, he clearly shows that Judas' greed was accompanied by the other disciples myopia. He wrote, but **when his disciples saw *it*, they had indignation,** (Mat 26:8a). In spite of Judas's influence over the disciples in this matter, it was over-ridden by Jesus. **Then said Jesus, "Let her alone: against the day of my burying hath she kept this. For the poor always ye have with you; but me ye have not always."**

It was unlikely that Mary thought anything of Jesus' impending death and burial because if she had, she probably would have saved some of the ointment. But she poured it all out. Her act was clearly a spontaneous act of love. It is in the opinion of this writer that Mary brought the box with her with an idea similar to that Judas had expounded, to sow a seed into the ongoing efforts of the ministry. Nevertheless, being overcome with love and devotion, she expended it all on the one deserving it the most, her Lord. Jesus recognizing the authenticity of her act, lovingly received it and used it for a memorial to her for all eternity. **Verily I say unto you, "Wheresoever this gospel shall be preached in the whole world, *there* shall also this, that this woman hath done, be told for a memorial of her."** (Matt 26:13) Miffed at Jesus' response to Mary's act of compassion, Judas left that party and joined the party of conspirators plotting the Lord's death. The chief priests were not only consulting to His death, but that of Lazarus also. Apparently the crowd from Jerusalem had made a pilgrimage of sort to the town of Bethany as much out of curiosity of seeing Lazarus alive as they were of seeing Jesus. In the midst of the curious were also new believers who come to the realization that Jesus was indeed the Christ. This, of course, incensed the chief priests even more and made even more their determination to extinguish the Light of the World. **The Pharisees therefore said among themselves, "Perceive ye how ye prevail nothing? behold, the world is gone after him".**

And Jesus answered them, saying, The hour is come, that the Son of man should be glorified. Verily, verily, I say unto you, Except a corn of wheat fall into the ground and die, it abideth alone: but if it die, it bringeth forth much fruit. He that loveth his life shall lose it; and he that hateth his life in this world shall keep it unto life eternal.
(Joh 12:23-25)

CHAPTER 13

The Servant is Not Greater
Than His Lord

> Now before the feast of the passover, when Jesus knew that his hour was come that he should depart out of this world unto the Father, having loved his own which were in the world, he loved them unto the end. (Joh 13:1)

After a feast such as the one honoring Jesus at Simon the leper's house, it would have been easy for Him to bask in the glory of such a celebration. It is human nature to relish being extolled, loved or honored. If anyone had a reason to undergo an ego boost, it was Jesus. In spite of the shadow of the cross, the honor bestowed upon him by his disciples would have been a very heartwarming event. With the cross looming, I am certain that Jesus took great pleasure from the display of love poured out by His friends. In a figurative manner, the disciples gave Him His flowers while he was yet alive. Nevertheless, the subsequent encounter showed a resolve in Him that could easily have been overlooked. Unlike the rest of us, who would have emerged from such a celebration with considerable boost of self confidence and feelings of importance, Jesus on the other hand was quite the contrary. Never missing a teachable moment, Jesus puts on display perhaps the greatest object lesson ever. **He riseth from supper, and laid aside his garments; and took a towel, and girded himself. After that he poureth water into a bason, and began to wash the disciples' feet, and to wipe *them* with the towel wherewith he was girded.** This example was a model to be followed in not only for the disciples of His generation, but also in the generations to come. What necessitated this lesson was not recorded by the evangelist John, but it was recorded by St. Matthew in chapter 20.

> **And he saith unto them, Ye shall drink indeed of my cup, and be baptized with the baptism that I am baptized with: but to sit on my right hand, and on my left, is not mine to give, but** *it shall be given to them* **for whom it is prepared of my Father.**
> **(Mat 20:23)**

As it turned out, the mother of James and John being the instigator, created a ruckus, so to speak, asking of Jesus to allow her sons positions of rank and authority in his coming kingdom. The other ten disciples overhearing the request became incensed at her boldness and apparent lack of regard for the rest of them. They had to be reminded that the purpose of the kingdom was to serve, not to be served. It was with that notion in mind that Jesus girded himself with the towel and began to wash the dirty, stinky feet of His disciples.

One of the most poignant depictions of the servant leader was described by Carter Woodson in his classic work "The Mis-Education of the Negro," as the writer commented on the futile practice of placing white leaders over black institutions. Woodson wrote, "The servant of the people, unlike the leader, is not on a high horse elevated above the people and trying to carry them to some designated point to which he would like to go for his own advantage. The servant of the people is down among them, living as they live, doing what they do and enjoying what they enjoy. He may be a little better informed than some other members of the group; it may be that he has some experience that they have not had, but in spite of this advantage he should have more humility than those whom he serves, for we are told that "Whosoever is greatest among you, let him be your servant."" Clearly, Woodson understood the idea of servant leadership as he related the leadership style of Jesus to an apparent contradictory style being manifested in the educational institutions he had the opportunity to evaluate. The tendency of self serving leaders is not confined to that of whites leading black colleges and schools tasked with the burden of educating blacks, but also in the churches.

The Armor-Bearer has become a staple in many churches. In addition to caring for the temporal needs of the pastor, he is the person who carries the pastor's bible and carefully places it on the pulpit as the pastor prepares to preach. Obviously, the pastor could easily perform this menial task for himself but out of respect and honor, the armor-bearer readily performs this function. It is a tradition in the black church which traces its biblical authority from 2 Kings chapter 2 describing the relationship between Elijah and Elisha. Elisha was a protégé of the Elijah and it was upon him that the anointing fell once Elijah was taken up to heaven in a whirlwind. When King Jehoshaphat made an enquiry regarding the presence of a prophet in the midst, Elisha was described in 2 Kings 3:11 as the one who poured water on the hands of Elijah, making reference to his service to the elder prophet. It is out of this tradition that the role of armor-bearer emerged. Though servile, it is still considered a position of honor. What sticks out in the mind of this writer is that those pastors who are the least deserving are the ones who are most likely to employ the use of an armor-bearer. Many years ago, my former pastor, the late Dr. Fred L Maxwell, considered an icon among the preachers of Orlando, having pastured for over half a century well into his nineties without an armor-bearer, had fallen and broke his hip. Myself, along with my brother in ministry Dr. Willie Caison now of Gainesville Florida, were called upon to assist our beloved pastor down the stairs each morning at nine o'clock am and return in the afternoon at six pm and assist him back upstairs the week following his release from the hospital and rehab. Both of us, being pastors ourselves considered it an honor to assist our mentor and spiritual father during those trying times and were prepared to continue as long as necessary. For the next four days we met at the parsonage diligently and performed what we considered a privilege. On the fifth day, we arrived at the parsonage to assist our mentor, but much to our surprise, at ninety-five years of age, he managed to get down the stairs by himself, thanked us, and informed us that we were no longer needed. His healing had progressed to the point where he felt comfortable navigating the stairs alone. He told us that although he appreciated our sacrifice, he could no longer be a burden to us. If there was ever a servant of God, who deserved an armor-bearer it was Dr. Maxwell, yet he was not inclined to employ one. Perhaps it was because of the multitude of protégés who sat at his feet, all willing to serve him in any way, and the difficulty in deciding one individual and not wanting to create an atmosphere of envy amongst his under-shepherds compelled this great man of God to forgo any air of pomposity. It was in like manner that Jesus found himself when the disciples were jockeying for position as to who would sit at his right and left hands in the kingdom. In other words, who would become his armor-bearer? While some pastor's utilization of the armor-bearer could be reasonable, as would have been the case of Dr. Maxwell, had he chosen to employ one, there are many examples where this practice has been taken to the extreme. I have observed some pastors, from mega-church to storefront; employ not only armor-bearers, but also entourages and security teams. It is quite easy to get besides oneself and allow the lofty position to go to one's head.

People have a tendency to venerate our pastors and rightly so. We are to esteem them for the work's sake and they are worthy of double honor, yet at the same time, we are to remember to humble ourselves and allow God to exalt us, not man. This was the reason that Jesus donned the towel and began to wash his disciples' feet. The purpose of the exercise was fivefold. **First** of all, He wanted to give proof of his love for them. **Having loved his own which were in the world, he loved them unto the end.** In spite of their numerous flaws and hang-ups, He never refrained from loving them. Just as Mary showed her love for Him by washing his feet, He showed His love for them by doing the same. What was most ironic in this encounter was the presence of Judas Iscariot who would later excuse himself to meet with his conspirators after this show of love. The disciples that truly loved him remained there to the end and were treated to the greatest lesson in spiritual growth possible while that deceiver Judas was engaged in his self-serving treachery. It is unimaginable how Judas could continue in his infamy after having experienced such a display of unmitigated love. The **second** purpose of the encounter was to demonstrate to the disciples the necessity of condescending to the needs of the people you are serving, knowing that this would be a needed quality for advancing the kingdom once he was gone. There would always be a need to reach down to a needy persons' level if one hopes to elevate that person to the next level of living. The **third** purpose of the washing of the disciples' feet was to show them that because of the treachery of one that he would not cast aside those that remained. Having co-signed Judas' outrage at the anointing of the ointment, calling it a waste, the disciples would have felt some consternation upon the realization of the magnitude of the treachery of

Judas. Such an act could easily have sullied the fellowship not only with their master, but also with each other, knowing that they all had sided with the traitor. Jesus wanted to assure them that their friendship was not subject to change because of their misguided passions. The **fourth** purpose of the washing of feet was to exemplify a spiritual cleansing. His exchange with Peter lends proof to this contention. **Peter saith unto him, Thou shalt never wash my feet. Jesus answered him, If I wash thee not, thou hast no part with me.** Peter was taken aback seeing His master condescend to such a menial position and was not quite ready to accept it. Jesus knew that Peter was not quite there yet and like us, needed this lesson in humility. Finally, the fifth purpose in this affair was to stress the absolute necessity of obedience to His will even when you don't understand the reason why? Before the night was over, everything would make sense to them all. However, at that moment, no one could fathom the depth by which their ordeal would take them. As Jesus instructed them on proper behavior in His absence, he stressed to them the importance of caring for each other while he was away. Once Judas went out, he was able to speak freely, knowing that His Father would soon be glorified. Jesus said to them, **"A new commandment I give unto you, That ye love one another; as I have loved you, that ye also love one another."** Don't love each other the way Judas showed his love with selfish ambition and hidden motives, but love completely, unashamedly. Recognizing that His departure would leave them in a quandary, the commandment to care for each other was urgently needed. Once Jesus reminded them of the message given to the Jews, that where he went, they could not follow, Peter responded, **"Lord, why cannot I follow thee now? I will lay down my life for thy sake."** Jesus answered him, **"Wilt thou lay down thy life for my sake? Verily, verily, I say unto thee, The cock shall not crow, till thou hast denied me thrice."**

CHAPTER 14

I am the Way

The philosopher believes you can think your way back, the indulgent believes you can drink your way back, the politician thinks you can spend your way back, the liberals think you can legislate your way back, the scientist believes you can invent your way back, the industrialist believes you can work your way back, labor believes you can strike you way back, the fascist thinks you can bluff your way back, the militarist thinks you can fight your way back, the bible says you can pray your way back, but Jesus says I am the way back, **I am the way, the truth and the life, no man can come to the Father but by me.**

--J. Vernon McGee

Observing the disciples anxiety, Jesus took the opportunity to allay their fears. **Let not your heart be troubled.** Knowing that His hour was quickly approaching and He would no longer be with them; Jesus knew that his remaining moments must not be wasted, so he immediately went from teaching mode to parent mode in order to prepare them for his departure. This change in mode was characterized by Bruce in his classic work *The Training of the Twelve,* as of a "dying parent to his little ones." The tone went from a master instructing his disciples to that of a dying father to his soon to be orphaned kids. Most recently, a colleague of this writer lost her husband to death and she had to explain her husband's passing to their newly orphaned five year old daughter. It was with the same simplistic tenor used by my colleague to her little one that Jesus deployed with His disciples.

"**Little children**........Let not your heart be troubled:" In the words of Bruce, "He knows our souls in adversity." As my friend was tasked with the duty of explaining the death of her five year old daughter's father to the grieving child, Jesus was tasked with the duty of preparing his little ones of the need to persevere in the face of mounting affliction and doubt. When Thomas questioned Him on how they were to go on without Him, Jesus replied, "**I am the way, the truth, and the life: no man cometh unto the Father, but by me. If ye had known me, ye should have known my Father also: and from henceforth ye know him, and have seen him.** Philip, was just as baffled as Thomas when he asked Him, "Lord, **shew us the Father, and it sufficeth us.**" The reason they continued to be baffled was because they constantly ignored or failed to apprehend the message repeated by Jesus that His Kingdom was not an earthly kingdom but a spiritual kingdom and not of this world. They were still anticipating a temporal kingdom with all the trappings of political power and prestige. Finally, it was about to dawn on them that a temporal kingdom was not what He meant. When Jesus spoke of going away, in their minds, it was about going on a pleasure cruise or some trip to an exotic city and leaving them behind. Now as it became clear that He was speaking of His death, they were more perplexed than ever. In spite of their ignorance, one thing is commendable concerning Thomas and Philip; at least they were willing to be taught, which is more than can be said for many modern day church members. The same can be said of post-Christian America, where the zeal for the things of God is quickly waning. Because of this phenomenon, she has lost her standing in the world and very soon will cease to be a great power. For America, there is, however a way out of this malaise and His name is Jesus.

Jesus was never about missing a teachable moment. As any good parent with a child, when the teachable moments arrive, be ready to expound and expand the truth and wisdom needed by the child. Jesus wanted to assure them that his death, although it would appear to be a great calamity was merely an access point where he would go and prepare for them the rewards due all of His children. His word of solace was as much a word of exhortation to remain faithful as it was as a reminder of the reward given to the faithful.

"**In my Father's house..**", was as much a reminder of His assignment as it was for them a word of encouragement. In a sense, He was reminding them that this world was neither His home, nor theirs. They were all on assignment and His portion of the assignment was coming to an end. His children on the other hand, would be given the task of completing that assignment. He reminded them of the works he had performed in their midst and used those reminders as proof of the assignment. **Believe me that I *am* in the Father, and the Father in me: or else believe me for the very works' sake. Verily, verily, I say unto you, He that believeth on me, the works that I do shall he do also; and greater *works* than these shall he do; because I go unto my Father.** He promises the disciples that as impressive as the works that He performed were, the works of the servants would exceed those of their master.

His comforting words gave them assurance that they would have the power to carry out the assignment. The key to tapping into this power was **first** of all faith in Him; He **that believeth on me,** and secondly, prayer. It was very important for the disciples to continue developing a disciplined and effective prayer life. **And whatsoever ye shall ask in my name, that will I do, that the Father may be glorified in the Son. If ye shall ask any thing in my name, I will do *it.*** The admonition to act and pray in faith in His name does two things, it assures them that they will be enabled to do the works that he had done and also that they are assured that they will able to exceed him. Just as the He was able to draw and convince heathens, so should they. Just as He was able to heal the sick, so will them. Just as He healed with the hem of His garment, Peter was able to heal with his shadow and Paul was able to heal with the touch of a handkerchief. Divine enablement is the engine that drives the gospel train. Jesus knew that any attempt to do the works of God without divine enablement was a lesson in futility. Although it was always His purpose to depart, it was never His purpose to leave them unprepared to continue the mission.

In the midst of their grief concerning His departure, Jesus continued to counsel and instruct them on proper behavior in his absence. Their tears, anxieties and fears gave testimony to their love for Him; He bids them to show their love for Him in a more productive way. **If ye love me, keep my commandments.** In essence, what Jesus was communicating to them was, the world will know that you are my disciples if you love one another, show me that you love me by your obedience to my commands. Not only did their faith and obedience warrant the promise of answered prayer but it also warranted the comforter who is the Holy Spirit. **And I**

will pray the Father, and he shall give you another Comforter, that he may abide with you for ever; What is interesting about the comforter is it is translated from the Greek word *parakletos defined by Strongs as;* An *intercessor, consoler:* - advocate, comforter. Just as Jesus Himself comforted them, he would send another like Himself to comfort them in the person of the Holy Spirit. Follow the conduct of the Spirit and you shall have the comfort of the Spirit. The Holy Spirit's job is to be Christ's advocate with them and all subsequent disciples in the earth. When Jesus was with them, he spoke for them, but upon His departure, He would not leave them defenseless. While they had Jesus with them he exhorted them to do their duty; but in His absence he leaves another to do the same, though silently. The Messiah was the promise of the old testament and was fulfilled in the person of Jesus the Christ, the parakletos was the promise of the new testament and would be fulfilled in the person of the Holy Spirit.

CHAPTER 15

I am the True Vine

> I am the true vine, and my Father is the husbandman. Every branch in me that beareth not fruit he taketh away: and every *branch* that beareth fruit, he purgeth it, that it may bring forth more fruit. (Joh 15:1-2)

The fallout created by the sons of Zebedee, James and John wanting special positions in the kingdom, continued well into the evening following the Passover feast. Not only precipitating the most urgent teaching on love and humility characterized by the washing of the disciples feet, it also lead to the discourse of the promise of the Holy Spirit. Knowing His work with the disciples was woefully unfinished; Jesus decided to take the teaching even further. Perhaps sensing that maybe the previous lesson on Pneumatology (the study of the doctrine of the Holy Spirit), was over their heads, Jesus decided to use a practical analogy to enable them to better grasp the teaching on that subject and what it would take to allow Him to bring about the necessary changes in their most despicable lives. The lesson to the eleven is the lesson paramount to all believers wanting to fulfill their purpose and become more fruitful Christians.

How He began the discourse; **"I am the true vine,"** was a dead giveaway that what is to follow would be life changing. Again, He uses the phrase "I AM" pointing to His Deity. What is interesting here is that he uses the analogy of the vine to teach an important spiritual lesson. What makes this significant for me is that my own grandfather, the late Benjamin Maxwell was a farmer and raised citrus trees. He taught this

106

skill to my uncles who in turn taught us, (at least they attempted to teach us). One of my uncles, Oliver, nicknamed "Hickey" was exceptional at this craft and was able to produce a citrus tree with three different varieties of fruit on one tree. The technique he used was grafting "bud-wood" into the into the outer bark of the tree and the sap which flowed through the outer bark would sustain the engrafted bud-wood causing it to grow a branch of the variety of the bud-wood in addition to the branches of the original root. Once the new budded branch was established, he would remove original branch whose fruit was less desirable in favor of the new engrafted variety which produced a more favorable crop. The original seedling had a sour root stock which was able to withstand more harsh growing conditions but the fruit from it was not usable. The preachers and theologians with a similar background in citrus farming look at the text and understand the allegory immediately, where those from a less agrarian culture may be a bit more perplexed. Jesus, being the master teacher that he was again deployed the natural to explain the supernatural.

In this passage, He not only describes the abiding life but He identifies Himself as the vine and His Father, as the husbandman, (the dresser of the vine, the caretaker, and horticulturist) and not just a vine, but the "True Vine," suggesting that if a true is emphasized, then there must be a false vine. The key to understanding the abiding life is stated in the phrase in verse 5, **"ye are the branches"**. When we view the Christian's life as a branch connected to a tree or a vine, then the futility of trying to live this life can be overcome. There are five keys to understanding the abiding life which can be observed in the relationship of the branch and the vine. These keys are absolute dependence, deep restfulness, much fruitfulness, close communion, and absolute surrender.

ABSOLUTE DEPENDENCE

In the first place, it is a life of absolute dependence. The branch has nothing, it just depends on, and receives everything from the vine. The branch is hopelessly dependent on God alone. Andrew Murray wrote, "absolute, unalterable dependence upon God alone is the essence of the religion of angels. It should also be that of men also."

The vine does the work, the branch enjoys the fruit. The vine sends its roots into the ground to get nourishment and moisture, converts it into sap and directs the life sustaining sap to the branch.

In the Christian life and in the work of the Church, this is exactly what Jesus wants us to understand. Christ desires that in all our work, the responsibility for results is on Him. He does it by sending down the Holy Spirit which nourishes us like the sap is sent from the vine nourishing the branch. The question arises, how can you be absolutely dependent on God? By becoming absolutely helpless in one's self. Absolute dependence on God is the key to power in Christian work, and the key to living the abiding life.

ABIDING RESTFULNESS

Secondly, the life of the branch is not only a life of complete dependence, but also of abiding restfulness. Imagine for a moment that the branch could speak. He would say to the vine, "thank you vine for giving me nourishment. Thank you for giving me moisture in the summer heat, preventing me from wilting." If the branch could speak, that would be his mindset, because at harvest time, when the owner came to pick the grapes, the branch would not have to care, because if there was not anything good, the vine would be blamed not him. The blame is always on the vine. If you would be a true branch of Christ, the living Vine, just rest on Him. Let Christ bear the responsibility. As a child of God, we must learn to allow the Lord Jesus to work through us. Rest in Christ, who can give wisdom and strength. The writer to the Hebrews wrote it this way.

> Heb 4:3 For we who have believed do enter into that rest; even as he hath said, As I sware in my wrath, They shall not enter into my rest: although the works were finished from the foundation of the world.

> Heb 4:4 For he hath said somewhere of the seventh *day* on this wise, And God rested on the seventh day from all his works;

> Heb 4:5 and in this *place* again, They shall not enter into my rest.

An abiding rest could be described as staying put in a constant state devoid of self effort. The Christian worker experiences the abiding life not only by being absolutely dependent on God and engaging in abiding restfulness but also being abundantly fruitful.

ABUNDANTLY FRUITFUL

Thirdly, the branch teaches a lesson of being abundantly fruitful. The Lord Jesus Christ repeated the word fruit many times in the parable. You are commanded to not only bear fruit, but much fruit. Joh 15:8 Herein is my Father glorified, that ye bear much fruit; and *so* shall ye be my disciples. Since this directive is given in the imperative, it is obvious that it is possible to accomplish. If it is possible to accomplish, then why are so many Christian workers to barren? Because they have ignored the lesson of the vine.

When we observe a grape vine laden with plump juicy grapes or an orange tree whose branches are bending downward by the weight of its fruit, one does not wonder why there is an abundance of fruit. We already know. The vitality of the vine is evidenced by the abundance of the fruit. Good healthy trees produce beautiful, delicious fruit. It has nothing to do with the branch. It has everything to do with the vine or tree. Though the fruit dangle from the branch it is the effort of the vine which produced it. The branch merely wears it like an ornament. This is like a kept woman and a sugar daddy. The rich sugar daddy earns all the money, but the kept woman wears the diamonds and jewels. The amount of jewels she wears in public testifies to the acumen of the sugar daddy. What is the fruit of the disciple, more disciples? When a believer is being fruitful, he is leading others to Jesus Christ by sharing the Gospel message of His atoning death on Calvary's cross, How He was buried in a borrowed tomb, and on the third day arose from the dead. That is how a believer is being fruitful. What then could prevent fruit from coming? By not allowing the sap of the Holy Spirit to supply the branch or by trying to nourish the branch with some source other than God Himself. We can preach Dr. Phil or Oprah, we can share the message of philosophy and social justice, but people will not get saved. When we allow the Holy Spirit to have its fruit in us, then we will have our own fruit and our fruit will remain. Every soul is a potential grape of the heavenly vine, so we must not only bear fruit but much fruit and more fruit. The abiding life is achieved by absolute dependence of God, in a state of abiding rest while being abundantly fruitful. This commandment can not be kept unless we remain in Close Communion with God.

ATTACHED COMMUNION

Fourthly, the life of the branch is a life of close communion. We ask ourselves, what is the branch to do? In the words of Christ, the word "Abide" is a primary verb which means to *stay* (in a given place, state, relation or expectancy). If your life is to be an abiding life it has to be like the branch, attached continually to the vine, abiding every minute of the day. The branches are in close communion, in unbroken communion, with the vine. The abiding work is the work of the heart. It is the work of the heart clinging to and resting in Jesus. How can you accomplish this is the hustle and bustle of everyday life? First of all, make a contract to put aside other work, secondly, find a place to secretly commune in prayer, thirdly, take time to be alone with Christ, and finally, get into the Word and let the Word get into you. Like the branch which is absolutely dependent on God, abidingly restful in Him, abundantly fruitful through Him and for Him, closely communing with Him, we must be absolutely surrendered to Him.

ABSOLUTELY SURRENDERED

Finally, the life of the branch must be a life of absolute surrender. This is serious statement. 1 Kings 20 gives a perfect example of absolute surrender.

> **And Benhadad the king of Syria gathered all his host together: and *there were* thirty and two kings with him, and horses, and chariots: and he went up and besieged Samaria, and warred against it. And he sent messengers to Ahab king of Israel into the city, and said unto him, Thus saith Benhadad, Thy silver and thy gold *is* mine; thy wives also and thy children, *even* the goodliest, *are* mine. And the king of Israel answered and said, My lord, O king, according to thy saying, I *am* thine, and all that I have. (1Ki 20:1-4)**

Because of Ahab, King of Israel's sin, Ben Haddad had marched onto Jerusalem to take his Kingdom away. He offered an ultimatum to Ahab to give up completely. Because of Sin, Ahab lost his Kingdom and was given the ultimatum of absolute surrender, which he complied. We are given the ultimatum to give absolute surrender to Jesus. But unlike Ahab who was a king and became a slave by his surrender, when we surrender to Christ, we become Kings. When we live the abiding life we are no longer slaves to our sin nature but we become rulers and joint heirs with Christ. This was such an important truth, that Jesus chose to teach it in his final session.

CHAPTER 16

Don't Be Offended

These things have I spoken unto you, that you should not be offended. <u>Joh 16:1</u>

As Christ continued to prepare his disciples for dealing with the world in His absence, He paints a very vivid picture of the abuse and ridicule that they should expect to endure in His name. Basically, He is telling them, "don't take it personal." Jesus knew full well that the people, who hated Him, would take their hostility out on those representing Him. Just as He was our substitute incurring the wrath of God over our sin, the disciples would become His substitute incurring the wrath of man because of His imputed righteousness. For He who knew no sin became sin for us that we might become the righteousness of God in Him. Jesus could not allow the eleven to possibly think that it would be easier on them because He would be gone. On the contrary, He knew that the Holy Spirit who would come and indwell them would convict the world of their sin and would only provoke more wrath upon those who were his witnesses. He wanted them to expect trouble. He never wanted them to get into a pattern of ease and lack of discernment because their very lives were at stake. He said to them, "**They shall put you out of the synagogues: yea, the time cometh, that whosoever killeth you will think that he doeth God service.**" At that moment, He was referring to the religious people, the church folk, not to mention the heathen. He knew the disciples should expect the most vitriolic reaction from those people who should have known better. He also explained to them why they should expect such hostility from the religious folk they encounter saying, **"And these things will they do unto you, because they have not known the Father, nor me."** His most poignant explanation could not allay their fears because they were still sorrowful over talk concerning his departure. He further explained why he must leave them, **"Nevertheless I tell you the truth; It is expedient for you that I go away: for if I go not away, the Comforter will not come unto you; but if I depart, I will send him unto you."**

With the cross looming in a matter of hours, Jesus knew that this encounter must account for something because their tests would soon be upon them and their hour of temptation was drawing nigh. He explained to them that the same comforter which would sustain them was also the reason for the harsh treatment from those they would encounter for the gospel's sake. Concerning the Comforter's effect on the world, He said, **"And when he is come, he will reprove the world of sin, and of righteousness, and of judgment: Of sin, because they believe not on me; Of righteousness, because I go to my Father, and ye see me no more; Of judgment, because the prince of this world is judged."** He needed them to endure the initial temptation to abandon their task, because once the Holy Spirit would come upon them, He would empower them to carry out the task. Until that time, they needed more encouragement from Him. His attempt to convince them of the benefits of his departure was not so successful because as we will see in the next substantial encounter, like many subsequent disciples, myself included, they would crack under pressure. In spite of the assurance from Jesus Himself, the disciples could not fathom the glory to be revealed.

History has shown us that Jesus' warning to his disciples proved to be more than prophetic. Throughout the ages, men have suffered for His names sake. The first disciples at the hand of the religious folk as much as the pagans. Even in our day, the persecution continues. In some parts of the world, to name the name of Christ will cost you dearly, even your natural life. In the U.S., no one would dare openly harm a follower of Jesus physically, but the attacks are still present. Today, it is quite common for individuals to be harmed economically for naming the name of Jesus and being a witness for Him in the world. Anyone who openly opposes public policy which flies in the face of sacred scripture, that person will be vilified, ostracized and made to look like a fool. Countless individuals have lost their jobs because they made public stands against the popular culture on issues such as abortion and gay marriage. Many years ago (1995), I wrote an article published as an op-ed in one of our local newspapers, The Advocate, entitled, "For the Sake of the Children." This article was decidedly pro-life and prompted a reader to curse me out in public. The young woman had had an abortion and somehow convinced herself that I was referring to her. Although her words were hurtful to me, they paled in comparison to her actions against her unborn child. Recently, one of my favorite sports casters, Craig James was fired as an analyst on ESPN for taking a stand on traditional marriage as he campaigned for a political office a few years earlier. When he made his statements defending marriage as a sacred union between one man and one woman, he was not an employee for the network nor was he speaking as such. Nevertheless, because he took a stand for Christian values in the public arena, his career as a sportscaster was derailed. The gay advocacy groups went after him with their pitchforks and the network capitulated under their criticism. Similarly, Brendan Eich, the inventor of Java Script was forced to resign as CEO of Mozilla, the parent company of internet service provider Firefox, for making a small contribution to the 2008 ballot initiative in California banning same sex marriage. His stance was the same stance voiced at the time by then candidate Barack Obama and former Secretary of State Hillary Clinton, who have since evolved in their thinking. If you are reading this book in any digital format, thank Brendan Eich. The ballot initiative won, by the way, by an overwhelming majority. Persecutions and assaults against people who align themselves with the cause of Christ and take a public stand will not abate. He warned us two thousand years ago that this would happen and when it does, it should come as no surprise.

These things I have spoken unto you, that in me ye might have peace. In the world ye shall have tribulation: but be of good cheer; I have overcome the world.
(Joh 16:33)

CHAPTER 17

Glorify Thy Name

These words spake Jesus, and lifted up his eyes to heaven, and said, Father, the hour is come; glorify thy Son, that thy Son also may glorify thee:
(Joh 17:1)

Following the farewell address to His disciples in the foregoing encounter, Jesus gave what was probably the most detailed of His recorded prayers. Not to be confused with the prayer commonly referred to as "The Lord's Prayer", which was actually the model prayer, it was this prayer which signified His office as our great High Priest. The prayer itself is most significant for as much the timing as it was its content. **"The hour is come,"** the hour for which he was born into the world as the son of man had come, where the Son of God would be sacrificed as the lamb of God, who takes away the sin of the world. An hour appointed by the Father for which the Son always anticipated yet never wanted to hurry. An hour filled with joy yet also full of grief and angst. Within the hour, He would be betrayed into the hands of the agents of Satan. Knowing this, He still went to His Father in prayer.

He began the prayer by praying for Himself. **"Glorify thy Son,"** He said. Not the self serving and self seeking prayer we are so accustomed to making. Knowing what was about to transpire, the son of man needed divine enablement to accomplish the task but He never mentions the impending sufferings. Later, He would pray to let the cup of suffering pass from Him, but now, in this High Priestly prayer, He makes no mention of it. Perhaps it is His intention to let the saints of subsequent generations know that in order to receive your glory, you must endure your suffering. It serves as a warning to this modern day theology of prosperity that requires no sacrifice, no suffering, nor sickness.

What is also interesting in this prayer is that Jesus speaks in past tense, as if He had already completed His assignment and ….. **"I have glorified thee on the earth: I have finished the work which thou gavest me to do."** …. yet the cross was before Him. After praying for Himself, His focus was turned to the benefit of the disciples. Just as Jacob blessed his sons upon his death and Moses blessed the twelve tribes upon his death, Jesus was now blessing the apostles upon His death. **"I have manifested thy name unto the men which thou gavest me out of the world:"**

What we are given here is the ministry of intercession. Of all the gifts to the church, this is probably the most unappreciated. Interestingly enough, Jesus makes a distinction as to whom He intends to be the recipient of the blessing in the prayer. He states, **"I pray for them: I pray not for the world, but for those whom thou hast given me; for they are thine:"** It is this line in the prayer that the hyper-Calvinists use to buttress their doctrine of election, interpreting the words of Jesus to mean that He did not die for the world, but only for the elect. We will debate that minor point in another book, but clearly Jesus wanted to emphasize his love, grace and protection on behalf of His disciples. **"Sanctify them in the truth: thy word is truth."** But He did not stop there, He continued with a focus not only on that current group of disciples but also on all the ensuing disciples who would come to believe because of the ministry efforts of those. **"Neither for these only do I pray, but for them also that believe on me through their word;"** The ability to go before God on behalf of someone who lacks the power or will to go to Him for themselves is powerful and must be utilized to a greater extent. In every church, it is the prayer meeting that is probably the most ill attended event on the schedule, but is the most needed.

My old seminary professor, the late Dr. Samuel Gordon often used the adage, "more prayer, more power, much prayer, much power, mighty prayer, mighty power, no prayer, no power." Jesus knew that the effectual, fervent prayers of the righteous availeth much, which is why He gave us this most perfect tool and He expects us to use it for His glory. Oswald Chambers, the author of My Utmost for His Highest, referred to intercessory prayer as the "Ministry of the Interior" because it undergirds all the other activities related to the service of Christ. It is the ministry of the interior that Jesus is telling us not neglect, because in prayer we will assure our victory. In fact, intercessory prayer is so powerful; we can keep a sinner from dying and going to hell. In His first epistle the Evangelist John taught us: "**And this is the boldness which we have toward him, that, if we ask anything according to his will, he heareth us: and if we know that he heareth us whatsoever we ask, we know that we have the petitions which we have asked of him. If any man see his brother sinning a sin not unto death, he shall ask, and** *God* **will give him life for them that sin not unto death. There is a sin unto death: not concerning this do I say that he should make request. (1Jn 5:14-16)**" As believers, we are given the authority to go before God on behalf of a sinner and ask God to give them more time to repent before they die in their sins. That is a power that must be utilized more in this our day. A personal benefit of intercessory prayer is clearly shown in Job 42:10, which was written, "**And the LORD turned the captivity of Job, when he prayed for his friends: also the LORD gave Job twice as much as he had before.**" The abundance came as a result of his intercession on behalf of others.

CHAPTER 18

The Hour Is Come

When Jesus had spoken these words, he went forth with his
disciples over the brook Cedron, where was a garden, into the
which he entered, and his disciples. And Judas also, which
betrayed him, knew the place: for Jesus ofttimes resorted thither
with his disciples.
(Joh 18:1-2)

Hardly a moment had passed before the serenity and sanctity of the
prayer was interrupted by the mob. Judas, the betrayer, led the band to
the very spot where the prayer for his very soul had been rendered which
initiated perhaps the most dramatic encounter of all. This arrest would be
like none other. Upon approaching Jesus, He asked the officers, "**whom
seek ye?**" Their immediate reply was, "Jesus of Nazareth." His response
should have been a dead giveaway that something apocalyptic was about
to occur. When He responded, "**I am He**", the entire band fell to ground
as if responding to the force of a mighty wind. So that the scripture might
be fulfilled, "that none would be lost", Jesus submitted to the arrest and
convinced the mob to allow his disciples leave. But then, in typical Peter
fashion, **Simon Peter having a sword drew it, and smote the high
priest's servant, and cut off his right ear.** If the band had not gotten
a clue as to what was about to transpire, they should have seen the light
when Jesus touched the servant's ear and healed it. Once Jesus was bound,
the disciples fled and sought cover, not realizing that there was a covering
over them that could not be removed or annulled.

Betrayal is a very serious thing and brings with it very serious emotions. Like rats fleeing a sinking ship, the other eleven disciples fleeing must have touched the heart of Jesus, but nothing like the betrayal of Judas. When Judas approached the Lord with the band to take Him, Jesus called him "**friend**" as sign to Judas that it was not too late to repent of the treachery and ask for forgiveness. Many of us have been party to betrayal whether the victim or perpetrator. The eleven disciples fleeing was as much a betrayal as was the treachery of Judas. They were under divine protection and never in any danger, yet they fled out of fear. But Judas, with evil in his heart betrayed the Lord with a kiss. Even though it was too late for Judas to abort the arrest, it was not too late for him to abort his fatal damnation.

Many years ago, during my darkest hour, I had backslidden and was struggling with a cocaine addiction and hiding it from my wife. One of my closest friends, out of envy I suppose, revealed to my wife my secret. On many occasions, I had attempted to confide in my wife and ask for her forgiveness and support, but in my shame, I could never muster up the guts to tell her the truth. In her mind, I was this perfect husband and I did not want to sully her opinion of me. If only she had known the truth. My pride prevented me from seeking the support I truly needed from the only person to whom It really mattered. I also knew that unless I could confess my weakness to my wife, I would always be in bondage to my addiction, an addiction that was getting stronger as the weeks went by. Nevertheless, I kept my problem hidden.

There was an innate harboring of jealousy on the part of my friend because of his own addiction and misery. In his mind, I still had everything, while he had lost everything, his career, his car, countless tangible assets, and the respect of his family but most of all his self respect. Although we were partners in slime, I did a better job of masking my weakness than him. One evening, while my wife was singing my praises, my buddy could take it no more and revealed to her the very thing I wanted to tell her but lacked the moral courage to do. What my friend (whose name I am omitting from this book) meant to damage me, God allowed for my good. When Daisy confronted me with my friend's accusation, I felt a strange feeling of relief. In tears, I admitted what I had been doing to my wife, who ministered to me and helped me break the bondage of my addiction. After his betrayal, my friend (yes, I still call him friend) and his wife departed and Daisy and I talked it through. Although she was disappointed in me, she suspected something was amiss. I promised to never use drugs again, but I needed her to believe in me. We spent that night together in prayer, which was our dramatic encounter. By morning, my deliverance was complete. Since that day almost a quarter of a century ago, I have used no illicit drugs of any kind, nor have I drunk any brand of beer; there were no twelve steps, no meetings, no rehab, only an encounter with Jesus and the intercessory prayer of a believing wife.

The betrayal of Jesus had reached its climax, leading to His arrest, arraignment and trial. There was another trial taking place alongside His, it was the trial of Peter. Sometimes I wonder why the Lord Jesus chose the Apostle Peter to become one of his disciples. When you look at Peter, and what he became, you can only be amazed by what happened. Peter was this brash, tempestuous, ignorant fisherman whom the Lord used mightily for His glory and purpose. I am so grateful that Jesus chose a man so unqualified for spiritual things because I know he can use me too. Throughout scripture we can see countless cases where God chose to use the unlikely to do the remarkable. However, in every case a transformation had to take place in that person's life before the mediocre could do the magnificent. In making the transition from mediocrity to magnificence, a turning point has to take place. But before Christ could fill him with his Spirit and make a new man of him, he had to get his attention and break him. He had to be delivered of self.

Peter denied the Lord three times, and then the lord looked upon him. The look of Jesus marked the turning point. Peter's heart was broken. The terrible sin he had committed, the awful failure he had displayed and the depth to which he had fallen suddenly was exposed to him. One awful look. Peter went out and wept openly. Until you are broken and self is exposed as the vermin that it is there will never be a turning point. Your Spiritual life will never take on the vitality that God intends until it does. You will always hinder the perfect will of God for your life until you say goodbye to self. Peter's restoration would be possible because of his repentance. Repentance means to turn away from sin to God. The point where one turns marks the beginning of your restoration. I could only imaging how Peter must have felt that night after that awful look and the sound of the rooster's crow. Having witnessed the Lord being hauled off from judgment hall to judgment hall; and having witnessed his crucifixion even from afar brought shame and despair that must have wrecked his soul. "My Lord is gone; my hope is gone; and I have denied Him, God have mercy on me," must have been Peter's words. How that must have gnawed at Peter's soul. We can never fathom the depth of Peter's humiliation, but that was the turning point and the change.

The similarity of Jesus' trial to that of Peter's in that His ordeal was as much an attack by Satan as was Peter's. The difference was, Peter's trial did not take place in an earthly court of law. Satan went to the Father and obtained permission to sift him like wheat. The sifting was a process of testing the character and commitment of Peter. Peter of course failed his test but Jesus restored him anyway. Now, Satan has returned his attack on the Lord Jesus Christ himself. The initial attack began pre-natal through the agency of Herod in his attempt to slay every male child under the age of two. It was picked up in the wilderness as he prepared to begin earthly His ministry. In every attempt by Satan to thwart the design of God and redemptive plan of God, Jesus responded as the obedient Son of God and triumphed over him. His true character and commitment was clearly revealed in every test and through every trial.

CHAPTER 19

His Humiliation and Sacrifice

Then Pilate therefore took Jesus, and scourged *him*. And the soldiers platted a crown of thorns, and put *it* on his head, and they put on him a purple robe, And said, Hail, King of the Jews! and they smote him with their hands. Pilate therefore went forth again, and saith unto them, Behold, I bring him forth to you, that ye may know that I find no fault in him. (Joh 19:1-4)

Though this trial had the same spiritual implications as the previous it was through a mock judicial proceeding that Satan would attempt to carry it out. Through this kangaroo court encounter we will see Satan in his attempt to use human agents, once again to confound the redemptive plan of God, but we are reminded that through His providence, all things work together for the good, to those that love God and are the called, according to His purpose. In these verses notice the human agents Satan used in his attempt to nullify the plan of redemption and avoid his fate in hell. As we look at those agent and their characteristics, we might learn to identify those traits in others that Satan uses to shipwreck the souls of men and the purposes of God in our own lives. The agents identified in the text as stooges of Satan are Caiaphas the High Priest, Annas, his Father-in-Law, the Jewish Council, and Pilate, the Roman Governor. Each played a part in the trials of Jesus, but most importantly each possess some character traits that play right into the hands of Satan. By recognizing those traits in ourselves, we can reduce our susceptibility to being played by the enemy of our souls, which is Satan.

THE CRUELTY OF CAIAPHAS

> **And led him away to Annas first; for he was father in law to Caiaphas, which was the high priest that same year. Now Caiaphas was he, which gave counsel to the Jews, that it was expedient that one man should die for the people. Joh 18:13-14**

Although in this chapter, Annas was introduced first, it was a remark made previously by Caiaphas the acting High Priest, in Chapter eleven that sets the tone for the injustice that was to befall Jesus.

> **Then gathered the chief priests and the Pharisees a council, and said, What do we? For this man doeth many miracles. If we let him thus alone, all men will believe on him: and the Romans shall come and take away both our place and nation. And one of them, named, Caiaphas, being the high priest that same year, said unto them, Ye know nothing at all, Nor consider that it is expedient for us, that one man should die for the people, and that the whole nation perish not. Joh 11:47-50**

This incident occurred as a result in the growing popularity of Jesus among the people following the resurrection of Lazarus from the grave. The religious leaders were so fearful of not only losing their influence with the people but also of losing their autonomy with the Romans in case a popular uprising would occur if Jesus were to institute a secular kingdom and overthrow the Romans. It was the cruel Caiaphas who came up with idea to kill Jesus to placate the minds of the Romans and keep his power. People will do anything to keep their perks and privileges. The murder and mistreatment of innocent people take place all over the world just because someone in authority does not want to relinquish that authority to another. Caiaphas figured if he could get rid of Jesus, he'd have little to worry about from the Romans. Killing and innocent man was not beneath him because he was just plain cruel and that was just the type of person that Satan is looking for to forward his ambitions. Anyone who's motivation is to further their own ends by any means necessary is just playing into Satan's hand. Whether it is cheating in an election or assassinating a political opponent it is the same cruel trait Satan loves to utilize in men.

THE COMPLICITY OF ANNAS

Jesus answered him, If I have spoken evil, bear witness of the evil: but if well, why smitest thou me? Now Annas had sent him bound unto Caiaphas the high priest. Joh 18:23-24

After Jesus was arrested, he was taken first to Annas who in turn turned him over to Caiphas, who as High Priest, arraigned and charged him in the religious court of the Jews. The reference to being smote made by Jesus in verse 23, came about during that proceeding. Usually the Jewish court did not meet during the wee hours of the morning, but in their haste to do away with Jesus while most of the people were asleep, the court broke its own rules and met after midnight to carry out its injustice. Almost as an afterthought, the Holy Spirit included verse 24 reminding the readers that it was Annas who delivered Jesus bound and shackled before Caiaphas. Any mistreatment committed by anyone after that point made Annas an accomplice to the injustice. Any part we play in allowing the mistreatment of another, God will hold us accountable. Whenever injustice and immorality is present and we allow it to happen without speaking against it makes us an accomplice. Though Annas did not directly participate in the proceedings, he knew what would occur and did nothing to prevent it. If we have prior knowledge that a crime or act that is unlawful or unholy will occur and be silent about it, God will hold us accountable. Unlike Nicodemus, who was part of the Religious council and spoke out against the trumped up charges and conspiracy to get Jesus, being overruled, he left the council in disgust. Annas was not a part of the council or any of the legal proceedings but his approval was apparent, numbering him among the pawns of Satan.

THE CONTRADICTION OF THE COUNCIL

Then led-they Jesus from Caiaphas unto the hall of judgment: and it was early; -and they themselves went not into the judgment hall, lest they should be defiled; but that they might eat the passover. Joh 18:28

Caiaphas and Annas were individuals involved in the trials of Jesus but the main culprits were the entire Jewish Religious Council. Their hypocrisy was so blatant it was laughable. Having tried Jesus in their religious court on trumped up charges, knowing they did not have the legal authority to condemn a man to death, forced them to go to the civilian gentile court of the Romans. Having taken Jesus before the Roman praetorium to be tried before Pilate the Governor, they thought they were too good to step foot inside the Roman Hall of Justice on the day of Passover. According to their tradition, if any Jew were to enter into a gentiles court he would be ceremonially unclean and not eligible to take the Passover meal. Therefore, after waking up Pilate in the middle of the night and forcing him to convene his legal proceeding, they had the audacity to refuse entrance into the hall where the proceedings would take place. Forgetting the fact that the charges were a sham, they thought they were too good to enter a Roman facility and soil themselves. As Jesus would say, woe to you, you hypocrites.,, They strain at a gnat but swallow a camel' Anyone who ignores the Spirit of the law and contort the letter to serve their own end is a hypocrite and is worthy of condemnation. The hypocrite, or one who wears a mask contradicting their true character is another who is displaying the character of Satan. Murdering an innocent man was not defiling to them but entering into a Gentile court was.

THE COWARDICE OF PILATE

Pilate saith unto him, What is truth? And when he had said this, he went out again unto the Jews, and saith unto them, I find in him no fault at all. Joh 18:38

As far as Pilate was concern, Jesus had broken no Roman Law and posed no threat to Rome, therefore he was prepared to let him go but the Jews cried out for his blood. Fearing Caesar, Pilate relented and went along with the Jews. After attempting to rid himself of, the matter and suggesting that they choose between Jesus and a malefactor named Barrabas as the one who would get pardoned. It was the custom of Rome to allow one prisoner go free each year for whatever reason just to placate the local populace. Pilate assumed they would vote to allow the release of Jesus over the terrorist and insurrectionist Barrabas, but the Jews chose otherwise and demanded the release of Barrabas and the crucifixion of Jesus. Pilate, after already pronouncing the innocence of Jesus, went along with the murdering mob and allowed the murder of an innocent man, just to hold his position. Unlike Caiaphas and Annas, whose motivation was just plain evil, or the council members who were motivated by greed and jealousy, Pilate was simply to much of a coward to do the right thing and stop the injustice. He too has gone down in history as on the biggest pawns Satan has ever used. Cowardice is one of the most frequently used character traits employed by Satan. He loves to use the moral coward just as much as he loves using the mass murderer. The coward can be more effective because there are more of them. If you are a coward you are playing in Satan's hands. If you are too cowardly to say no to drugs, Satan has you where he wants you. If `you are too much of a coward to take a stand, you have fallen into Satan's trap.

The cruelty of Caiaphas, nor the complicity of Annas, not even the hypocrisy of the Council, nor the cowardice of Pilate would prevent God's plan from manifesting itself. Satan thought he could convince Jesus to forgo the Father's will in the garden of Gethsemane, but he did not succeed. He thought he had him when they nailed him to the cross. I could see Satan gloating when they lifted Jesus onto the cross. But I remember what Jesus said, "If I will be lifted up from the earth, I will draw all men unto me." When he hung on the cross from the six to the ninth hour and the sun refused to shine, Satan just knew that he had won. When Jesus said, "Father, into thy hands I commend my spirit, It is finished," Satan's gloat beamed like the dawn, but then, the earth went into a violent rage, and nature begin to mourn, I could just hear someone say, "surely,he must be the son of God." When they buried him a borrowed tomb, Satan was certain that he had won, but that was on a Friday afternoon.

CHAPTER 20

His Exaltation

And he stooping down, *and looking in,* saw the linen clothes lying; yet went he not in. Then cometh Simon Peter following him, and went into the sepulchre, and seeth the linen clothes lie, And the napkin, that was about his head, not lying with the linen clothes, but wrapped together in a place by itself. Then went in also that other disciple, which came first to the sepulchre, and he saw, and believed.
(Joh 20:5-8)

The next encounter comes from a text of scripture that describes the events of resurrection morning at the empty tomb. We all recognize the fact of the resurrection. It is capstone of Christianity. It is the event that proves the truth claims of Jesus. That he is the virgin born Son of God, God in Flesh, the creator of all things, and in whom all things exist. In whom we have redemption through his blood, *even* the forgiveness of sins: Who is the image of the invisible God, the firstborn of every creature: For by him were all things created, that are in heaven, and that are in earth, visible and invisible, whether *they be* thrones, or dominions, or principalities, or powers: all things were created by him, and for him: And he is before all things, and by him all things consist.

The encounter at the empty tomb presents to us another enigma, the folded napkin. "**And the napkin, that was about his head, not lying with the linen clothes, but wrapped...**" We find the disciples entering the empty tomb. Having discovered the linen clothes lying haphazardly as if someone undressed hurriedly and discarded the clothing wherever, much like my son Lawrence, when he changes his clothes, they are subject to be flung all over the room. The linen clothes were discarded in a similar manner. But the napkin was not thrown, it was folded. There is a lesson to be revealed in the folded napkin. The Oriental would get the message of the folded napkin immediately. We, on the other hand need some explanation. Peter, when he looked into the sepulcher, he understood immediately the meaning of the folded napkin.

In the Orient, when a great man sits down at feast, his servants will tend to his needs. These men usually had full beards, no eating utensils and a full course meal had the potential to get quite messy. Once he has had his fill, he would take a linen napkin and wipe his hands, beard and the rest of his face. Then he would discard the napkin in a haphazard way. Much like the linen clothes found in the empty tomb. But if the master was not finished he would take his napkin and fold it neatly and put in place so that the servant would know that the master was not through and had every intention to return to his place. When Peter looked into the tomb, I could hear him say, **the napkin is still folded!** Seeing the folded napkin probably triggered many memories and a floodgate of emotions. Peter probably remembered Jesus' words, "**Let not your heart be troubled.**" I am certain that much of the anxiety experienced since observing his Lord's arrest, scourging and crucifixion was now abated. "**In my Father's house are many mansions:**" There was now a peace within the soul of Peter as he recalled every reassuring word spoken by Jesus. Words triggered by the mere presence of the folded napkin. "**I go to prepare a place for you.**" The fear and doubt was now being replaced with a blessed assurance that whatever challenge might befall him, he would be able to bear it; the greater works that lay before him, he would be able to accomplish it because the napkin is still folded.

> **Then went in also that other disciple, which came first to the sepulchre, and he saw, and believed. For as yet they knew not the scripture, that he must rise again from the dead. Then the disciples went away again unto their own home. But Mary stood without at the sepulchre weeping: and as she wept, she stooped down, *and looked* into the sepulchre, And seeth two angels in white sitting, the one at the head, and the other at the feet, where the body of Jesus had lain. And they say unto her, Woman, why**

weepest thou? She saith unto them, Because they have taken away my Lord, and I know not where they have laid him.
(Joh 20:8-13)

Often overlooked at the empty tomb encounter was Mary Magdelene (along with the other women) approaching the tomb of Jesus expecting to dress His body for permanent entombment. Joseph of Arimathea and Nicodemus had hastily prepared the body of Christ for burial because of the impending Sabbath. After the Sabbath had passed, the women were going to finish the job. Though John only cited Mary Magdelene, we gather from the other Gospel writers that it was a full contingent of women who were there. Obviously they were present all along because they were aware where and how the body was laid.

And the women also, which came with him from Galilee, followed after, and beheld the sepulchre, and how his body was laid. And they returned, and prepared spices and ointments; and rested the sabbath day according to the commandment.
(Luk 23:55-56)

Mary Magdalene was singled out by John because it was she who ran to tell Peter of the empty tomb. It was this Mary who had been delivered from demonic possession. Her gratitude and love for Jesus was demonstrated by her attendance to his final needs. (so she thought) Because she had been forgiven much, she loved much. (Lk7:37) Mary was not a theologian nor was she a member of his inner circle. She did not get the privilege of being trained at His feet like the twelve. She did not host Him in her home like Mary of Bethany. All Mary of Magdela knew was that she was once tormented by seven demons and Jesus cast out those demons, restoring her sanity and giving her life purpose. Jesus had become the central focus of her life and serving Him was the most important thing she could do. Now she finds herself at the tomb of her Lord and he is not there. She knew He should have been there but she could not find Him.. She ponders, what have they done with my Jesus?" Although she was not a member of the inner circle, she still identified herself as a disciple of Christ and was never too far away from Him. Like so many others who make that identification, sometimes we lose all the evidence of His presence in our lives. Many things can cause us to loose sight of our Savior. By examining Mary and her interactions with the other disciples, we can see how one might loose sight of the risen Lord, but also how one might overcome this lost contact and reconnect with Him. In looking at the text, we see three things that explain why a disciple could disjoin himself from Jesus and how these same three factors can be a bridge in repairing and strengthening our relationship with Him which are; mental cognition, emotional volition, and divine communication..

MENTAL COGNITION

Mental cognition has to do with knowing something or someone because of personal experience. The ability to associate subsequent events to previous evidence requires mental cognition. Jesus had taught on many occasions about his death and subsequent resurrection. The scriptures testified of the sufferings and redemption of the Messiah. (Hos 6:2, Ps 16:10, Is 53:10, Is 26:19) Therefore, the disciples were without excuse. Mary never allowed anything to separate her from Jesus, but she and the other women were not privy to the private teachings of Christ concerning the resurrection. The twelve were told on many occasions by Jesus Himself that he would rise again from the dead. But they did not want to hear that. (John 16:17) The truth of the Gospel was not received by them because it did not fit what they wanted to hear. The twelve did not believe the teachings of Christ Himself concerning the resurrection. So they certainly did not believe Mary Magdalene's report of the empty tomb. Only John the beloved, upon inspecting the empty tomb believed, but the inspection was the result of skepticism, not faith. Even after finding the empty tomb, they failed to connect the event to what Christ had already told them. The disciples all went back home.

So the disciples went away again unto their own home. Joh 20:10

It is a dangerous thing to disengage one's mental process in the apprehension of the things of God, If you are truly one of His, you will apply line upon line and precept upon precept until a more clear picture of the Savior is seen in your mind. Failure to develop mental cognition will result in loss of power, loss of faith, reversionism, damaged witness and a woefully inadequate view of God's plan of redemption. When you obscure and ignore the facts concerning the Lord, the Spirit may quit striving with you and you lose your anointing and never know it. Like Sampson and King Saul, God's anointing had departed from them and they did not even realize it. Unlike the disciples, Mary's response to a missing Jesus was further probing not retreat.

EMOTIONAL VOLITION

Volition is the actual exercise of the power which the mind has of considering or forbearing to consider an idea. Mary Magdalene's soul purpose in life was to follow Jesus. The constancy and fervency of her affection to the Lord Jesus was without question. Although the disciples possessed more facts concerning the resurrection, when confronted with the empty tomb, except for John they still manage to disbelieve. They exercised their volition by going back home. Peter once said, "Lord I'll die for you, I'll never leave you." Yet he left him prior to the crucifixion, and again after the resurrection. Mary Magdelene, on the other hand stayed at the sepulchre, even after Peter and John were gone. Why? because there her Master had lain, and there she was likeliest to hear some tidings of him. She did not have all the answers, but she felt that if there was going to be some answers, it would be where she knew Jesus should have been. Where there is a true love to Christ there will be a constant adherence to him, and a resolution with purpose of heart to cleave to him. This good woman, thinking she had lost him, yet, rather than desert him, remained by his grave for his sake, and continued in his love. She not only exercised mental cognition in evaluating the situation as she saw it. She was not satisfied with her limited understanding and sought out the truth. Where there is a true desire of acquaintance with Christ there will be a constant attendance on the means of knowledge. Her fervency was evidenced by her tears. She stayed there weeping, and those tears loudly bespoke her affection to her Master. Those that have lost sight of Christ have cause to weep; she wept at the remembrance of his bitter sufferings; she wept for his death, and the loss which she and her friends and the country sustained by it. Still she did not retreat, she willed herself forward. She wept to think of returning home without him; wept because she did not now find his body. Those that seek Christ must seek him sorrowing. But don't cry for Him, cry for yourself.

But Mary was standing without at the tomb weeping: so, as she wept, she stooped and looked into the tomb; Joh 20:11

As she wept, she looked into the sepulchre hoping to see something that would bring her solace. When we are in search of something that we have lost we look again and again in the place where we last left it, and expected to have found it. Some time ago, a customer left his wallet in my store. His license, credit cards and many valuable items were in the wallet. The very next morning he returned to the most likely place to find it. The exercises of emotional volition will often times accompany tears. But weeping must not hinder seeking. Though she wept, she stooped down and looked in. I am certain Peter, John and the other disciples also wept but they did not hang around to find any answers. They possessed all the mental Cognition or head knowledge to ascertain that He had risen indeed, but their volition was to go home and have a pity party. Not so with Mary Magdalene.

DIVINE COMMUNICATION

Joh 20:12 and she beholdeth two angels in white sitting, one at the head, and one at the feet, where the body of Jesus had lain.

Mary's devotion was about to pay off. The first part of this divine communication came about when she encountered the two strangers. They were angels, messengers from heaven, sent on purpose, on this great occasion to honor the Son and grace the solemnity of His resurrection. As the angels announced his birth in Bethlehem, again they are given the charge of announcing his resurrection. The fact that there were two of them was also significant. For out of the mouth of two witnesses this word would be established. They were in white, denoting, their purity and holiness. The best of men standing before the angels, and compared with them, are clothed in filthy garments. The angels were compassionate in their inquiry concerning Mary's grief.

And they say unto her, Woman, why weepest thou? Joh 20.13

The question arises, "why did they rebuke her for grieving?" As far as Mary was concerned she had the right to grieve and no other response seemed appropriate to her. None know, but those who have experienced it, the sorrow of a deserted soul, that has had comfortable evidences of the love of God in Christ, and hopes of heaven, but has now lost them, and walks in darkness; such a wounded spirit who can bear? There are many saved folk who live for a brief time in a fog; the fog of indifference, the fog of disbelief, the fog of despair, and like myself, the fog of addiction, Mary was in such a fog, but it was about to be lifted as she turned to see who had called out to her.

Jesus saith unto her, Woman, why weepest thou? whom seekest thou?. Joh 20.13

By exercising mental cognition and emotional volition, Mary was being rewarded with divine communication. She had placed all her trust in Jesus and now he was gone, she had a right to be grief stricken. She had witnessed Him being nailed to a rugged cross; she saw Him hanging there from the sixth to the ninth hour. She was a witness to his suffering as He died a criminal's death and had every right to be in grief. When they placed Him in a tomb, she thought she had lost Him, yet still she sought him out until she found him again. In her most dramatic encounter with the savior, He was calling out to her.

CHAPTER 21

If You Love Me

After these things Jesus shewed himself again to the disciples at the sea of Tiberias; and on this wise shewed he *himself.* There were together Simon Peter, and Thomas called Didymus, and Nathanael of Cana in Galilee, and the *sons* of Zebedee, and two other of his disciples.
(Joh 21:1-2)

The disciples final encounter was somewhat anti-climactic. Many of the the previous encounters had taken place in or around solemn assemblies, from the feast days, Sabbaths, weddings and of course funerals. Now we find a departure from the past pattern and see them having returned to the grind of their everyday life, the life of the regular fishermen. Here they quickly dispensed of all their previous teachings, including the lesson of the folded napkin. With no thought of the things of God, they commenced doing what they knew best, fishing. Unfortunately, something many men who are called of God to do a task, yet choose to do otherwise, they found something out. Until you fulfill your obligation to the Divine, your earthly pursuits will avail you nothing.

> **Simon Peter saith unto them, I go a fishing. They say unto him, We also go with thee. They went forth, and entered into a ship immediately; and that night they caught nothing.**
> **(Joh 21:3)**

What has become the testimony of countless preachers of the gospel and ministry workers who delayed entering into the Master's service, that none of their ventures were fruitful until they responded in obedience to His commands. Peter and his cohorts had fished all night and caught nothing. That would be the case every night until they heed the Master's call. It is never a good idea to remain idle for too long, so returning to one's life's work is not in itself a bad thing, especially when you are awaiting a more definitive order from above. So that complacency does not set in, it is good to occupy yourself until the master comes. Nevertheless, if you have not predetermined to heed the call when it comes, subsequent success will be extremely laborious. Since there needed to be a reminder of the blessings of obedience, Jesus orchestrated this encounter. It was not as dramatic as the others, but absolutely necessary none the less.

As the fishing boats returned to the shore that morning after a night of futility, there was a strange silhouette standing on the shore. The stranger shouted from the distance, **"Children, have ye any meat?"** After their negative reply, **he said unto them, "Cast the net on the right side of the ship, and ye shall find,"** They immediately complied with the suggestion of the obscure stranger and to their surprise there was an abundant haul gathered into the net. This success probably triggered the memory of John recalling some time ago when Jesus suggested they launch out into the deep after a dismal night of fishing and caught a slew of fish. **"It is the Lord,"** cried out John. From one hundred yards away, he could not see his face, but he just knew it was Jesus. Peter heard him and also knew it was Jesus. He girt about his fisherman's cloak and jumped into the water. By the time they arrived to the shore, Jesus had a fire going, and breakfast was already started. With the catch that was just hauled in, there would be more than enough. When Christ originally called Peter to forsake his nets and follow Him, he did it immediately and was reminded here, what happens when the words of Jesus are heeded.

> **Now when he had left speaking, he said unto Simon, Launch out into the deep, and let down your nets for a draught. And Simon answering said unto him, Master, we have toiled all the night, and have taken nothing: nevertheless at thy word I will let down the net.**
> **(Luk 5:4-5)**

Again, he submitted to the word of Jesus with great results. Furthermore, he remembered when he saw Christ walking on the water he said; *"Lord, if it be thou, bid me to come unto thee"* **Matt 14:28** At the voice of Christ he walked on the water. All of these great memories rushed back into Peter's mind which compelled him to swim two hundred cubits to meet his Master. Before long, the encounter turned into a potluck breakfast. They were all dining on fish and bread.

While celebrating with the disciples in their final earthly encounter, Jesus asked Peter, **"lovest thou me more than these?"** What was interesting in this dialogue, Jesus asked, **"do you love me…."** Using the Greek word 'agapao', an expression of the highest form of affection or Godly love. Peter's response was an anemic, **"Yea, Lord; thou knowest that I love thee,"** using the Greek 'phileo', which is commonly translated to mean "brotherly love," clearly inferior to the Godly love expressed by Jesus. In spite of the apparent lack of total commitment by Peter, Jesus still reinstates him, telling him to, **"Feed my Lambs."** Indicating a charge to minister to and nurture the most tender of disciples. Jesus asked him a second time, **"Simon, lovest thou me?"** Again, using the word 'agapao', and again eliciting the same inferior response from Peter, **"Yea Lord, thou knowest that I love thee;"** Again using the word phileo in his response. Jesus accepts his response, but this time He tells him to **"Feed my Sheep."** This statement is directing him to minister to the maturing sheep. When I studied this text many years ago for the first time I was expecting Jesus to ask the third time using 'agapao' and eliciting a positive response from Peter using 'agapao', but to my surprise, Jesus said, used the word 'phileo' the third time and I was totally taken back by that. That's when it dawned on me. Without the an indwelling of the Holy Spirit, it is impossible for feeble men such as myself and Peter to love the way God loves, because God is love and the fruit of His Spirit's indwelling is love. So, when Peter was grilled the third time and Jesus having lowered his expectations, Peter was grieved by that and replied, **"Lord, thou knowest all things; thou knowest that I love thee." Jesus saith unto him, "Feed my sheep."** There was a lot more to this conversation than just the dialogue reinstating Peter which was not recorded by John. Shortly after the initial encounter at the shore, the attention turned to the other disciples when they were given further instructions. And Jesus came and spake unto them, saying, **"All power is given unto me in heaven and in earth. Go ye therefore, and teach** all nations, baptizing them in the name of the Father, and of the Son, and of the Holy Ghost:" and "preach the gospel to every creature. He that believeth and is baptized shall be saved; but he that believeth not shall be damned." Furthermore, "And that repentance and remission of sins should be preached in my name among all nations, beginning at Jerusalem. And ye are witnesses of these things." But most importantly, "Feed my Sheep."

In the last earthly encounter the disciples were given their marching orders, the great commission. Those marching orders have not been rescinded. Evangelize and preach the gospel, that people might get saved, make disciples, that they might grow in grace and reproduce, while not neglecting the preaching of repentance, calling out sin and being faithful witnesses to His goodness and His mercy. Jesus knew that sin would be the cancer that would weaken the power in the church. He envisioned the church as an open door to heaven. Dr. Brookins wrote, "what is promised to them is available to us, and the promise is, an open door to faithful service."

The End

BIBLIOGRAPHY

All scripture utilized in this book is from the King James Version (KJV) unless otherwise noted.

1. Brookins, Dr. Larry A., *Seven Things that God Hates & Seven Letters to Seven Churches, Bloomington, IN, Authorhouse Publishers 2010*

2. Bruce, A.B., *The Training of the Twelve, 1871*

3. Bureau of Census, *The 2011 Statistical Abstract of The USA: Income Distribution.*

4. Chambers, Oswald, *My Utmost for His Highest,* Urichsville, OH, Discovery House Publishers, 1935

5. Earle, TH.D. Ralph, *Word Meanings in the New Testament,* Grand Rapids, MI, Baker Book House, 1989.

6. Evans, TH.D., Anthony E., *The Promise, Chicago, Il. Moody Press, 1996.*

7. Glover, Dr. William L. *Justice: God, Nations, and Systems,* North Fort Myers, FL. Faithful Life Publishers, 2010.

8. Haney, Elissa, *The Jonestown Massacre, The Ministry of Terror, Infoplease.com 2010.*

9. Hembree, Ron, *Word Pictures From the Bible, Goodyear, AZ., Quick Study Publications*

10. Josephus, Flavious, *Antiquities of the Jews,* Word Press, Public Domain

11. Josephus, Flavious, *Wars of the Jews,* Word Press, Public Domain

12. Lewis, C.S., *Mere Christianity,* New York, NY, MacMillan Publishing Company, 1943.

13. Maxwell, D.D., Fred L., *Where is Thy Brother, Lake Mary, FL., Accord Books, 1990.*

14. Meyer, Rev. F.B., *Jeremiah,* New York, Fleming H. Revell Company, 1894

15. Ryrie, TH.D. Charles C., *Biblical Answers to Contemporary Issues, Chicago IL. Moody Press, 1974.*

16. Strong, James, *New Strong's Exhaustive Concordance, Nashville TN. Thomas Nelson Publishers, 2001.*

17. Tozer, A.W., *The Knowledge of the Holy,* Camp Hill, PA. Christian Publications,1985

18. Williams, Don, *12 Steps With Jesus,* Ventura CA., Regal Books, 2004

19. Woodsen, Carter G., *The Mis-Education of the Negro,*

20. Wright, Fred H., *Manner and Customs of Bible Lands, Chicago, IL., Moody Press, 1953.*